MEAT FIRE GOOD

A Pitmaster's Guidebook

Perkins, Ramsey, Renner

Published by:

Elk Mountain Books
PO Box 21
Wilsonville, Oregon 97070
info@elkmountainbooks.com

ISBN Print Edition: 1461194512
EAN-13: 9781461194514

Elk Mountain Books titles are available for special promotions and premiums. For details contact:
sales@elkmountainbooks.com

Cover Art by Dani Ramsey Photography
© 2011, Dani Ramsey

dramseyphotography@gmail.com

Table of Contents

We dedicate this cookbook to our wives.

Vickie
Dana
&
Julie

You tolerate our toys, listen to our endless foodie blather, and let us to come to bed smelling of hickory smoke.

Thank you.

*"Cooking is like love.
It should be entered into with wild
abandon...or not at all."*
~ Harriet van Horne

Multi-Zone Fires

Single Zone

Spread the coals in an even layer across the charcoal grid, or all burners of the gas grill lit to the same heat.

For grilling, you would use a single-zone fire for steaks, chicken breasts, or any food that requires a short, hot cooking time. Only use a single-zone fire if all of the meat will finish and be served at the same time.

Even when grilling the types of meat mentioned above, I still like to keep a small "cool zone" at one end of the grill so I can move meat away from flare-ups, melt cheese onto my burgers, etc.

Two-Zone

A two-zone fire is created when your lit coals are spread over one-half to two-thirds of the grilling area.

This is ideal for most types of grilling, especially those foods that need to be seared on the outside, and cooked more slowly on the inside (steaks, spatchcocked chickens, pork tenderloins, etc.)

As mentioned, one benefit of a two-zone fire, when cooking for a crowd, is that you have a "warming area" for foods that are done, or nearly done, to stay warm while another batch is cooking.

Three-Zone

Your best heat control is achieved with a three zone fire, consisting of a hot zone, medium zone, and cool zone.

On the charcoal grid, rake half the coals into a double layer over one third of the fire box, and the rest into a single layer in the center. Leave the remaining third of the grid without coals.

Use the hot zone for searing, the medium zone for finishing, and the cool zone for keeping food warm until serving.

*"The only time to eat diet food
is while you're waiting for
the steak to cook."*
- Julia Child

ON THE HOOF

(Beef & Lamb)

Soy-Honey Flank Steak

Chimney Steaks

Flat Iron Chili Steaks

Perry's Perfect Steaks

"Da Best" Burgers

Cuban Burgers (Fritas)

Nigerian Suyas

Grilled Brisket Pizza

Smokey Tri-Tip

Doug's Mock Tri-Tip

Teriyaki Tri-Tip Sliders

Chris Renner's True Texas Brisket

Smokey Beef Ribs

Mexican Barbacoa

Bacon Weave Smoked Meatloaf

Salt & Pepper Tenderloin

Thai Beef Satays

Castilian Roast Leg of Lamb

Moroccan Whole Roast Lamb

Soy-Honey Flank Steak

½ C red wine vinegar
¼ C minced fresh ginger
1 Tbs salad oil
4 cloves garlic, pressed
Lime wedges (optional)

¼ C soy sauce
3 Tbs honey
1 tsp black pepper
2 lbs flank steak

In a gallon-size resealable bag, mix together vinegar, soy sauce, ginger, honey, oil, garlic, and pepper. Add steak (close bag) and turn to coat. Refrigerate 6-8 hours, turning several times. Let rest at room temperature for 30 minutes.

Drain steak; discard marinade. Lightly oil grill, and lay meat above a solid bed of hot coals (you can hold your hand at grill level only 1 to 2 seconds.)

Cook meat, turning to brown evenly, until pink in the thickest part for medium-rare (125°F), 5 - 6 minutes per side.

Transfer steak to a cutting board and garnish with lime wedges. Thinly slice meat across the grain to serve. Offer lime wedges to squeeze over individual portions to taste.

Rare - 120°F   Medium Rare - 125°F   Medium - 130°F

Serves 6

Chimney Steaks

So, my partner in smoke…and BBQ-Jedi, Chris Renner, told me about this method, and I had to grab a couple of steaks and try it out.

Amazing results!

I'm not sure what the exact temp coming out of the chimney was, but it was a LOT hotter than the coals under the grill.

You can use a "burger basket", the grill from a small bbq, or, like I did, a cheapie disposable grilling basket (I happened to have one handy.)

These were the juiciest steaks, with the best "crusts," that I've ever cooked.

'Nuthin' on 'em but a little salt and pepper.

Thanks Chris!

Flat Iron Chili Steaks

Flat iron steak is the American name for the cut known as Butlers' steak in the UK and oyster blade steak in Australia and New Zealand.

Once a "throw away" cut or, at best, ground into burger, upscale restaurants have recently begun serving flat iron steaks on their menus since a new method of cutting and presenting this steak was developed by researchers at the University of Nebraska and the University of Florida.

This steak has a deep, rich flavor, which makes it perfect as a stand-alone dish, or as part of a recipe...with the recipe below, it's my cut of choice for steak fajitas.

2 flat iron steaks, 1lb each
2 Tbs onion, minced
1 Tbs balsamic vinegar
1 tsp hickory salt
1/4 teaspoon black pepper

3 Tbs olive oil
3 cloves garlic, minced
2 ½ tsp chili powder
1 tsp smoked paprika

Season steaks with hickory salt and place is a gallon-size resealable bag. Combine marinade ingredients and pour over steak, turn to coat, and seal up the bag. Let stand at room temp for 10 minutes. Preheat grill for medium high heat. Remove steak from dish, reserving marinade.

Place meat on grill and allow to cook for 13-15 minutes. Brush often with reserved marinade during cooking process. When meat reaches desired "doneness," remove from heat and allow it to sit for a few minutes before slicing.

Serves 6

Perry's Perfect Steaks

To grill the perfect steak, you get what you pay for. Go with t-bone, rib-eye or NY strips. If you can find a butcher that ages their beef 30 days, you'll taste the difference.

3lbs NY Strip Steaks, 2" thick.   Coarse sea salt
Fresh ground black pepper   Steak Butter

Remove steaks from refrigerator 1 hour before cooking, pat dry and allow to rest at room temp. Oil your grill and heat to highest temp.

If you can hold your hand six inches above the grill and count to two, it's not hot enough!

Add some oak and/or pecan chips, about ¼ cup of each, to the coals 5 minutes before the steaks go on.

Steak Butter:

½ stick of sweet cream butter   1 Tbs lemon juice
¼ cup chopped Italian parsley   2 Tbs minced garlic
1 Tbs Worcestershire sauce   dash red pepper flakes

Melt butter, stirring to combine ingredients (set aside two tsp of parsley for garnish) and pour into a baking pan.

Cooking: place steaks on grill and cook until lightly charred (about two minutes.)

Don't move steaks until the first side is finished cooking, then use tongs to turn.

Flip steaks to second side and grill 2 more minutes.

Remove from the grill and place in baking pan, dredging both side in the steak butter.

Return steaks to grill, sprinkle each side with sea salt and pepper, and finish cooking – you're looking for an internal temp of 115f.

Once steaks reach that (2-3 additional minutes per side) move them back to the baking pan, dredge in butter again, and allow to rest 10-15 minutes at room temp.

To serve, drizzle a little of the butter and juice mixture (from the pan) onto your cutting board and slice steaks thinly across the grain.

Pour a little of the butter/juice onto a plate, top with a fan of steak slices, and spoon a bit more butter over the top.

Sprinkle with remaining chopped parsley and serve immediately.

Serves 6

"Da Best" Burgers

Fletcher Davis of Athens, Texas, is believed to have sold hamburgers at his café in the late 1880s, then brought them to the 1904 St. Louis World's Fair. The McDonald's hamburger chain claims the inventor was an unknown food vendor at that same World's Fair.

The hamburger bun was invented in 1916 by a fry cook named Walter Anderson, who later co-founded White Castle in 1921.

3 Tbs lemon pepper
1 Tbs paprika
½ tsp sugar
½ tsp fresh black pepper
1lb ground beef, 20% fat

1 Tbs ground thyme
1 tsp granular garlic
½ tsp seasoned salt
pinch cayenne pepper

Mix spices, except for salt, with ground beef about an hour before cooking, to allow flavors to marry.

Form 3 - ½ inch thick patties, slightly larger than the buns, and sprinkle with salt just before grilling.

Sear your patties on each side over a high heat until a crust forms. This should take about one to one-and-a-half minutes.

Move patties to a cooler part of the grill and cook another ten minutes, flipping once.

Serves 3

Fritas
(Cuban Hamburgers)

Recipe by Roberto Guerra

1 lb ground beef
½ lb ground pork
¼ C bread crumbs
3 Tbs minced onion
2 tsp salt
½ tsp black pepper
12oz curly fries, cooked

½ lb Cuban chorizo
1/4 C milk
1/3 tsp paprika
1 egg
1 tsp Worcester sauce
Six soft white rolls

Combine all the ground meat and chorizos. Soak bread crumbs in milk, beat eggs and add to the milk together with all the remaining ingredients.

Add to the meat mixture and mix well using the hands. Shape into six patties. Place them in the fridge for a couple of hours. Serve on toasted rolls topped with crisp-cooked shoestring fries.

There is a big difference between Cuban chorizo and Mexican chorizo. Mexican chorizo has a grainier texture and tends to fall apart when you split the casing where as Cuban chorizo has more of a solid sausage texture. Also, Cuban chorizo has no hot peppers, and is packed with lots of fresh cilantro.

Serves 6

Nigerian Suyas

Suya is a very popular grilled street food that I discovered on the streets of Jos, Nigeria, while "cruising" with the kids on Friday nights.

A bonfire was built underneath the remains of a chain-link fence, and, when the fire had burned to coals, strips of meat (labeled beef, but more likely goat or dog) were spread out on the "grill." One side was sprinkled with a tongue-scorching peanut and pepper rub, then the thin strips were flipped and given another dose.

2 pounds of lamb, cubed	2 Tbs dry roasted peanuts
1 Tbs cayenne pepper powder	2 Tbs smoked paprika
1 teaspoon ground ginger	1 teaspoon garlic powder
1 teaspoon onion powder	1 Tbs fine sea salt

Grind the peanuts into a fine powder (briefly pound them in a mortar and pestle; crush them with a rolling pin; or use a food processor). Be careful not to grind them into a paste. Stir all of the spices into the powder, mix well, and divide the peanut-spice mix into two parts, putting half in one bowl and half in another. Set the second bowl aside.

Dip and roll the meat in the first bowl of the peanut-spice mix, making sure the meat is completely coated. Allow the meat to marinate for one hour or more. Place the meat on skewers and grill over hot coals, until meat is done.

Sprinkle with the saved rub from the second bowl, and serve.

Serves 8

Grilled Brisket Pizzas

Leftover barbecue makes for tasty pizza toppings, and prepared pizza dough helps make these appetizers a quick and easy crowd pleaser!

Alternatively, you can make two family-sized pizzas instead of sixteen individual ones.

½ C extra virgin olive oil
2 pkg "ready bake" pizza dough
2 C shredded pecorino romano
4 C leftover brisket, finely chopped

4 clove garlic, minced
4 C shredded provolone
2 C Texas Brisket Sauce

In bowl, combine oil and garlic. Cut dough into eighths. On lightly floured surface, roll each piece into 4-inch circle. Brush with oil mixture. Pile hot coals to either end of your cooking area, leaving a 1/3 area in the middle with just a thin layer.

Place dough, oiled side down, on grill and cook until golden, about 5 minutes. Flip dough and brush each with 1 Tbs Texas Brisket Sauce (*pg 107*), spread 1/4 cup provolone cheese over the grilled side, and top with 1/4 cup brisket; sprinkle with pecorino Romano cheese.

Cover and cook until bottoms are golden and crisp, and cheese is melted, about 5 minutes.

Makes 16 "mini" (or 2 full-size) pizzas

Next Level: Check out Terry's from-scratch pizza dough recipe on our website, http://www.burninloveblog.com

Smokey Tri-Tip

2 (4-pound) tri-tips, trimmed
1 cup soybean oil
½ cup soy sauce
½ cup garlic powder
½ cup chopped fresh garlic

1 cup lemon juice
½ cup white sugar
½ cup black pepper
¼ cup seasoned salt
½ cup chopped dried onions

To make the marinade, mix all of the ingredients except for the beef in a large mixing bowl. Combine marinade and meat in a vacuum marinade tumbler and process, per the machine's instructions.

If you don't have a vacuum marinade tumbler, place the trimmed tri-tips in a plastic container and pour the marinade over. Let stand in the refrigerator for at least 12 hours (24 is better.)

Heat grill to medium temperature, using oak chips or pellets to smoke. Place tri-tips on grill at a 45 degree angle to establish grill marks and cook about 35 minutes, or until cooked to desired "doneness."

Remove the tri-tips from the grill and let rest about 2 to 5 minutes before slicing.

Serve on steamed stadium rolls, or over sticky Jasmine rice as bento, with your favorite sauce. I like a sweet chili sauce.

Serves 12-18

Doug's Mock Tri-Tip

Recipe by Doug Fairrington

My buddy Doug jokes that he's too cheap for tri tip! Luckily, he's a master griller and has had great results with applying the same cooking methods to cheaper cuts of beef, like chuck roast.

The key with these muscle cuts, he says, lies in taking as long as possible to get them to 145 degrees.

Use an herb/spice butter to help add moisture, and an instant-read thermometer, so you don't have to cut into meat to check for doneness, allowing valuable juices to escape.

2 - 4 lbs chuck roast, cut 2" thick
1 Tbs onion powder
1 tsp oregano

1 Tbs garlic powder
1 Tbs celery salt
Italian dressing

Steak butter
1 lb sweet cream butter
2 Tbs garlic powder
1 Tbs coarse black pepper

4 Tbs seasoned salt
2 Tbs smoked paprika

Marinade meat overnight in oil and vinegar based Italian dressing, remove from marinade, and blot dry.

Mix all spices and rub both sides of roasts, then let stand at room temperature for 1 hour.

Warm butter and add seasoned salt, garlic, paprika, and pepper, blending well. Cool slightly until spreadable.

Heat one side of your grill to high, and the other to low, and lightly oil the cooking grate.

Place meat on hot side of the grill, fat side up, and grill five minutes per side.

Move steaks to "cooler" side of the grill and turn off the hot side.

You can place a drip pan under it to catch the drips which will make a great gravy later.

With the grill on low cook for about 1 hour or until it reaches your desired doneness.

Remove roasts from grill, flip, smear with remaining steak-butter, and allow to rest 15 minutes to before cutting in 1/8 " slices across the grain.

Serves 12-18

Next level: Try these either of these last two recipes with our "Tri-Tip Sliders with Garlic Provolone Sauce" recipe at www.burninloveblog.com

Teriyaki Tri-tip Sliders

Teriyaki is a cooking technique used in Japanese cuisine in which foods are broiled or grilled in a sweet soy sauce marinade (tare in Japanese). The tare is traditionally made by mixing and heating soy sauce, sake or mirin, and sugar or honey. The sauce is boiled and reduced to the desired thickness, then used to marinate meat, which is then grilled or broiled.

4 beef tri-tips (2 lb/ea.)	2 tsp dry mustard
4 C soy sauce	1 C brown sugar
3 C thinly sliced onion	2 C sake
2 C mirin	4 Tbs minced garlic
4 Tbs thinly sliced fresh ginger	2 tsp pepper

Pour soy sauce, sugar, onion, sake, mirin, garlic, ginger, pepper, and mustard into 4 – 1 gallon-size resealable bags. Add one tri-tip to each bag, and seal.

Chill 24 hours, turning occasionally. Lay tri-tips on a lightly oiled grill over a solid bed of coals, turning every 5 minutes, until 125° to 130° on an instant read thermometer, or about 25 minutes.

Transfer tri-tip to a cutting board. Let rest about 5 minutes, and then cut across the grain into thin, slanting slices. Place 1-2 slices on a split potato roll, top with *Simple Tangy Coleslaw*, or pickled ginger, and serve.

32 Sliders

Chris Renner's True Texas Brisket

Recipe by Christopher Renner

In Texas, barbecue means beef, particularly untrimmed brisket, that's been slow-cooked over coals or wood in above ground smokers

No sauce is used before or during cooking. Pepper and salt are the most common seasonings, and a thick tomato-based sauce with a sweet and spicy taste may be served on the side of the barbecue meal.

Beans, potato salad and thick toasted white bread called Texas Toast are often added to the meal.

3 whole brisket, 12-14 lbs	6 C Renner's Amazing Brisket Rub
2 C Mustard glaze (see below)	6 C Oak wood chips

The night before you plan to begin cooking, rinse the briskets, and pat dry. Place the briskets in large disposable pans and generously apply Renner's Amazing Brisket Rub (*pg. 116*) to all meat surfaces. Refrigerate overnight.

Preheat charcoal smoker for half an hour. Soak the wood chips for half an hour in water. Drain.

Remove the brisket from refrigerator 1 hour prior to cooking and let stand at room temperature.

Mop the entire brisket with Mustard Sauce, then sprinkle with another light coat of black pepper.

Place brisket fat side up in a smoker at a preheated temperature of 200 to 225 degrees F.

Add 3 handfuls of pre-soaked Oak chips to preheated charcoal (should be at the gray stage).

After 3 hours, add another 3 handfuls of chips.

After 2 more hours, place brisket on 2 pieces of heavy-duty foil and seal tightly.

Continue to cook in smoker (or oven) another 2 to 4 hours, or until internal temperature reaches 190 degrees F.

Remove brisket from foil and let stand 30 minutes. Slice brisket against the grain into ¼ inch thickness.

Serve with warm Texas Brisket Sauce on the side. *(pg. 107)*

Mustard Glaze
1 cup yellow mustard
1 teaspoon ground black pepper
1 teaspoon sea salt

Mix all ingredients in a medium saucepan. Reduce heat to low and simmer for 10 minutes.

Serves 45-60

Brisket Tips

Preparing: If you have a frozen brisket, let it thaw in the refrigerator for 2 days to defrost thoroughly. One hour before you plan to begin cooking, take the brisket from the refrigerator.

Remove the plastic packaging, rinse brisket well with cool water, and pat dry.

DO NOT remove the fat; that will provide moisture and flavor as the brisket cooks.

Reheating: Spritz the meat with apple juice and add 1/8" of the same juice to the bottom of the pan. Cover tightly with foil and heat in a 200-250°F oven until warmed to your liking. Just before serving, brush on a thin layer of your favorite barbecue sauce to give the slices a nice sheen.

If you prefer to keep the cooked brisket whole and unsliced, wrap it in foil and refrigerate. Before reheating, open the foil and add some juice or broth as described above, and close the foil tightly.

Heat in the oven or smoker at 200-250°F until warmed to your liking, then slice and serve.

Resting Time: At a minimum, place the brisket on a rimmed baking pan, cover loosely with foil, and let rest 30 minutes before slicing. 60-90 minutes is better.

Brisket Yield: When you take into account the trimming of the brisket before and after cooking, plus the shrinkage that occurs during cooking, don't be surprised if you end up with a 50% yield of edible meat from a whole, untrimmed brisket.

That means 6 pounds of edible meat from a 12 pound brisket.

Depending on the brisket and the internal temp you cook it to, it may be as low as 40% or as high as 60%.

If you're cooking brisket for a party, figure 4-5 ounces of meat per sandwich or 6 ounces of sliced meat on a plate (8 ounces for hearty eaters). Using a 40% yield, just to be safe, a 12 pound brisket yields 19 4-ounce sandwiches or almost 13 6-ounce plate servings.

Burnt Ends: Traditionally, burnt ends sold in restaurants were the dry edges and leftover bits and pieces of the brisket flat after slicing, mixed with barbecue sauce. These morsels were highly prized for their intense, smoky flavor.

Today, famous barbecue joints like Arthur Bryant's in Kansas City can't meet the demand for burnt ends using leftover bits, so they make a facsimile by cubing fully cooked brisket flats, placing the cubes in a pan and smoking them for a couple of hours, then adding sauce and smoking for a couple more hours.

Another approach for making burnt ends is to separate the point section from the flat section after the flat is done, then return the point to the cooker for smoke for an additional 4-6 hours.

Chop the point, mix with barbecue sauce, and enjoy!

Chris Renner preps "a couple" of briskets.

Smokey Beef Ribs

Beef Ribs may not be the pit-master poster child that pork ribs are, but these "dinosaur bones" of beefy goodness make for awesome barbecue, and they're often a great deal at the grocery store, as well.

Like pork ribs, if done wrong they can be tough and stringy, but when done right they're tender, juicy and full of flavor.

Plan on about 3 ribs per person, and you'll have a full and happy crew!

6 full beef rib racks, trimmed   1 C Beef Rib Rub *(pg 117)*
3 C Beef Rib Mop *(pg. 124)*   3 C favorite bbq sauce
2 cans of beer

The night before cooking, rub beef ribs and wrap in plastic. Refrigerate 12-18 hours.

Place disposable pan, with beer, beneath the grill rack to catch drips and prevent flare-ups. Allow ribs to come to room temp, and Preheat grill and prepare for indirect grilling.

Place ribs on the hot side of grill, searing for 2-3 minutes on each side. Then move to "cool side" to cook indirectly.

Grill for 1 to 1 1/2 hours turning and mopping every 15 minutes. Serve with your favorite bbq sauce (warmed) on the side.

Serves 8-10

Mexican Barbacoa

The ancient tradition of barbacoa, which is where we get the word "barbecue," runs deep within the culture of Mexico.

In the original, Indian pit-cooking process, the meat was seasoned, wrapped in either maguey or banana leaves, then placed on a grill over a cauldron of water that is set over glowing coals in a pit about three feet deep.

This recipe uses chuck roast for South Texas style barbacoa, but you can even use a bone-in pork shoulder, too. No need to dig a hole with this recipe!

3 Lbs. Beef chuck roast	1 Qt cold Water
2 - Chiles Ancho	5 Cloves garlic
1 Large onion, quartered	2 banana leaves
2 Tamarind pods	2 Lg bay leaves
1 tsp cumin	3 Tbs Fresh cilantro, chopped
Mexican sour cream	

Preheat grill to high and toss on a small handful of hickory chips. Sear meat, in smoke, 10 minutes per-side until starting to char. Turn one side of grill off, and reduce heat of second side to medium.

Move the roast to the "off" side and barbeque, with indirect heat, for one hour, adding smoke every 15 minutes.

Drape 2 banana leaves over a "deep-dish" disposable pan, pressing to the bottom, then add a layer of chopped onion.

Remove roast from grill and place in the pan on top of the onion, then add the cold water, chiles ancho, tamarind, bay leaves and garlic, fold banana leaves over the top and secure with a couple of toothpicks.

Place pan, uncovered, in a pre-heated oven (425d) for 20 minutes.

Once simmering, reduce heat to 175d and cover the pan with foil. Let simmer ten hours, turning the meat 2-3 times.

(You'll be "stirring" the last couple of times.)

After 10 hours, give the tamarind pod a few good smacks and pick off the shell, the stem and the thick fibers that run down its length. Remove the seeds and add the gummy pulp to the pan. Add the cumin and simmer one hour more.

Then, fish out the bones, ancho chiles, bay leaves, and banana leaves.

Pour off half of the fluids, and place the pan, uncovered, back in the oven for about an hour to let the juices bake down and thicken. Stir frequently.

Just before bringing to the table, stir in most of the chopped Cilantro, and quickly top with dollops of Mexican sour cream.

Serve with your favorite guacamole, salsa, and hot tortillas.

If you're a true chile-head, roast some whole jalapeños over the coals, slice, core (to remove the seeds) and serve on the side.

Serves 10-12

Bacon Weave Meatloaf
with Blue Cheese

2 lbs ground sirloin
4 scallions finely chopped
½ lb blue cheese

1 lb bacon (to wrap)
1 tsp minced garlic
Bread crumbs to bind.

Mixed together all of the ingredients, except bacon, and add just enough bread crumbs to bind it together.

Weave bacon into a square mat, top with meat mixture and roll into a log, with bacon completely covering the outside. Tuck bacon around ends to cover.

Cook, in your smoker, at 225 with hickory smoke until the internal temp reaches 165 degrees (about 1 hour per inch of thickness.)

Typically, about 2.5 hours is right on target. To serve, slice into 1 inch rounds and serve on soft white rolls.

Serves 5

Salt & Pepper Beef Tenderloin

The whole beef tenderloin roast is sometimes called a "whole filet," a "filet mignon roast," or a "tenderloin tip roast." It's a long, tapered muscle located on the inside of the short loin, extending from the 13th rib to the pelvis. As the name suggest, it is one of the most tender cuts of beef you can prepare.

3 beef tenderloins, 4lbs each	1 C fine sea salt
3/4 C olive oil	6 Tbs black pepper
Crumbled blue cheese (garnish)	

Buy the tenderloins pre-trimmed, around 5-6 lbs each. Pre-cut 7-8 pieces of kitchen twine, each about 18" long, for each tenderloin. Fold the tail under the center section to create an even diameter, and tie up each tenderloin evenly with 8 pieces of twine. Trim any loose ends. Pat dry and sprinkle all sides with 1-1/2 tablespoons of salt.

Wrap in plastic wrap and let sit at room temperature for one hour. This step allows the salt to penetrate the meat and will help it cook more evenly.

Just before cooking, apply a thin coat of olive oil and sprinkle with a good amount of freshly cracked black pepper; sear over direct medium heat until well marked, about 20 minutes, turning a quarter turn every 5 minutes. Continue grilling over indirect medium heat until internal temperature reaches 135° for medium rare, 10-20 minutes. Remove the tenderloin from the grill and let rest for 5-10 minutes. Serve whole, or cut into ¾-1 inch slices.

Sprinkle with a little crumbled blue cheese, and serve warm.

Serves 12

Thai Beef Satays

Satay (SA-tay), a very popular shish kebab style dish that has long been popular in Indonesia and Thailand. It is most frequently associated with Thai food, where satay made from cubes of beef, chicken, or lamb may be dipped in a traditional peanut relish or sauce. Satays are grilled or barbecued over a wood or charcoal fire, then served with various spicy seasonings, like our Spicy Thai Peanut Sauce.

2 lb sirloin tips
2 Tbs red curry Paste
2 Tbs fish sauce

60 bamboo skewers
26 oz coconut milk
2 Tbs minced ginger

Cut sirloin into thin strips

In a medium saucepan, heat coconut milk with the curry paste. Stir until smooth and bubbling. Turn off heat. Add fish sauce and minced ginger. Stir well and pour into shallow dish. Add the beef, making sure each piece is well coated. Cover and refrigerate for six hours or overnight.

Soak bamboo skewers in cold water 2 hours before grilling to keep them from burning on grill. Thread meat onto skewers and over hot coals for 3 minutes on each side or until done.

Makes 32 skewers. 16 servings.

Castilian Roast Leg of Lamb

This is a popular dish around the north of Madrid, especially during the Christmas season.

2 - 6 lb legs of lamb (butterflied)   4 Tbs of olive oil
Freshly ground black pepper   Salt
2 tsp fresh thyme   4 cloves of garlic sliced
2 C of dry white wine   4 C of water
2 Tbs of wine vinegar   Juice of 1 lemon

Rub the lamb with half of olive oil, season it with salt and pepper and rub the thyme over the surface of the lamb. Let the lamb sit for an hour to absorb the flavors.

Put the white wine, water, vinegar and lemon juice into a pan and bring to the boil. Allow to cool. Make some slits in the leg of lamb and put some slices of garlic into them, baste with ½ of the liquid, and then rub the lamb with the rest of the olive oil.

Prepare grill. If you are using a charcoal grill, prepare the coals so that they are double layered on one side of the grill, and sparsely single layered on the other side of the grill.

If you're using a gas grill, heat the grill on high on all burners to start.

Place the lamb, fat side down, on the grill on the hot side. Sear one side for 4 minutes, then flip the lamb over to sear the other side for another 4 minutes. Then, if you are using a charcoal grill, move the roast to the less hot side of the grill. If you are using a gas grill, lower the heat to low.

You will want to maintain a temperature of 300-350°F. Baste again, and then cover the grill and let cook for an additional 35-45 minutes until a meat thermometer inserted into the thickest part of the roast registers 130°F (for medium rare).

Transfer to a cutting board with a well to catch the juices. Cover with foil and let rest for 10-15 minutes. Cut across the grain, 1/4 to 1/2-inch thick slices. Serve slices on a warm platter; pour meat juices over the slices.

Serves 18-20

Moroccan Whole Roast Lamb

Recipe by Dee Elhabbassi

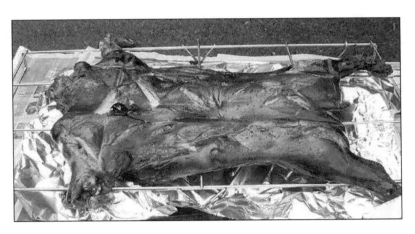

Abdellah and Dee Elhabbassi are the owners and Executive Chefs of my favorite restaurant, Dar Essalam *(translated House of Tranquility) in Wilsonville, Oregon*

This recipe is designed for use with La Caja China (the Cuban roasting box.) You can find instructions, online, for pit or rotisserie roasting whole lambs, as well.

---

1 - Grass-fed, three-month-old lamb around 36-40 pounds, skinned. As much surface fat removed as possible.

4 sweet onions, pureed	2 C fresh garlic, ground
2 C butter	2 C olive oil
Salt to taste	3 bunches cilantro, diced
¼ C cumin	½ C coriander
½ C paprika	2 Tbs fresh black pepper

Combine all chermoula ingredients and mix together over medium heat until it forms a paste. (*Chermoula is a Moroccan marinade.*)

Allow chermoula to set overnight.

Rub this mixture over the surface of the lamb making sure to get it evenly distributed, inside and out. Plan on allowing the chermoula to sit on the meat for 48 hours before you cook.

Place the lamb between the racks and tie using the 4 S-Hooks, inside the box, ribs side down. Connect the wired thermometer probe on the leg, be careful not to touch the bone. Cover box with the ash pan and charcoal grid.

Add 16 lbs. of charcoal for Model #1 Box or 18lbs. for Model #2 Box and light up.

Once lit (20-25 minutes) spread the charcoal evenly over the charcoal grid. Cooking time starts right now. After 1 hour (1st hour) open the box flip the Lamb over (ribs up) close the box and add 9 lbs. of charcoal. After 1 hour (2nd hour) add 9 lbs. of charcoal. Do not add any more charcoal; continue cooking the meat until you reach the desired temperature reading on the thermometer.

IMPORTANT: Do not open the box until you reach the desired temperature.

Fresh Lamb: Rare 140, Medium Rare 145, Medium 160

Dar Essalam *(www.daressalam.org)*

Succulent Swine

Pierna Criolla a Lo Caja China

Sweet & Spicy Pork Kabobs

Big Island Pork Kabobs

Asian Pork Sliders

Gracie's Luau Pork

Carolina Pork Ribs

Italian Porchetta Sandwiches

Bourbon Pork Tenderloin

Memphis Whole Pickin' Pig

Carolina Pulled Pork Sandwiches

Mom's BBQ Pork Chops

Peach Mojo Pork Shoulder

Sweet & Savory Bacon Wrapped Dates

Jalapeño Pepper Bombs

Pulled or Chopped?

At a Pig Pickin', the barbecue is likely going to be pulled from the bone and served in chunks. This "pulled pork" barbecue is mighty hard to beat. Add a finishing sauce if you like.

The barbecue served in a restaurant is usually chopped, and addition of finishing sauce during chopping is common.

If you decide to go the chopped route, be sure to remember that chopped and pureed ain't the same! Properly cooked barbecue is very tender and slicing is a tricky business when it is warm. Allow the barbecue to cool somewhat for consistent success.

Plunk it between a soft bun of white bread or eat it plain.

Always cook pork shoulders with the fat-cap up, and marinate, wrapped in plastic wrap, 12-24 hours.

Be sure to cook pulled pork to an internal temperature of 195d, and let rest 20-30 minutes before chopping.

Pork should be pulled while warm. My preference is to pull the pork after resting, and mix in some extra rub before serving.

To reheat, spritz with apple juice or drippings, cover tightly with foil, and heat in a 200-250°F oven or smoker, stirring occasionally, until warmed to your liking.

Pierna Criolla a Lo Caja China

Recipe by Roberto Guerra

This is the infamous recipe that Roberto used to defeat celebrity grillmaster Bobby Flay in their Miami Florida ThrowDown. It's one of my all-time favorite recipes!

1 - 8 lb. pork shoulder	8 slices bacon
1/2 lb. ham	1 bottle Malta*
1 cup guava shells*	1 cup Mojo (*pg. 125*)
1 cup prunes	4 tbs. Adobo*
2 cups brown sugar	2 Tbs sea salt

Debone and flatten meat so that it may be rolled. If the pork shoulder is very fatty, a small amount may be removed. Score fat well and marinate for a minimum of 12 hours in the Mojo, and Adobo. Sear both sides of roast over very hot coals until dark brown and charred in spots, you may add a small handful of apple-wood chips to the coals for a smoky flavor.

Remove roast to cutting board, and line unrolled roast with ham slices, bacon slices, prunes and guava shells. Roll meat carefully to keep the filling inside. Tie firmly with a butcher cord.

Cover with brown sugar and 1/2 bottle of Malta.

Cook for one hour in the oven at 325. At this point, turn the meat, cover with the remaining Malta and cook for an extra hour, or until you reach a meat temperature of 180. Allow to cool at least 30 minutes and cut into fine slices. Pour the drippings over the meat after slicing the meat.

Thanks Roberto!

Serves 15-18

These ingredients can be found at most Hispanic groceries, or can be purchased at www.lacajachina.com individually, or in a handy recipe pack.

Sweet & Spicy Pork Kabobs

2lbs boneless pork, 1-inch cubes
1 Tbs Worcestershire sauce
2 tsp black pepper
¾ C cider vinegar
4 Tbs lemon juice
2 cloves garlic, minced

¾ C olive oil
1 tsp dried thyme
½ tsp cayenne
¼ C sugar
1 Tbs oregano
1 tsp salt

Mix together first 11 ingredients, place in sealable bag and refrigerate 24 hours; thread onto skewers.

Grill over hot coals, basting with reserved marinade, for 4-5 minutes; turn and grill another 4-5 minutes. Sprinkle with salt, and serve.

Serves 6

Big Island Pork Kabobs

3 lb Pork tenderloin
3 clove garlic – minced
4 lbs whole mushrooms
4 tsp lime juice
3 Tbs minced parsley

3 C margarita mix
2 lg red bell pepper
¼ C butter - softened
1 teaspoon sugar

For marinate: combine margarita mix and garlic.

Cut pork into 1-inch cubes, place in a sealable plastic bag; pour marinade over to cover. Marinate overnight.

Blend together the butter, lime juice, Splenda, and parsley; set aside.

Thread pork cubes onto skewers, alternating with mushrooms and pepper, cut into eighths.

Grill over hot coals, basting with butter mixture, for 10-15 minutes, turning frequently.

Serves 6

If you're using bamboo skewers, soak them in water 20-30 minutes before using.

Asian Pork Sliders

Sliders (mini burgers) are one of my favorite barbecue appetizers. Quick, simple, and given to nearly unlimited variations, our guests can assemble their own favorite toppings from a pre-arranged "burger buffet" and all I have to do is flip the meat and serve.

The intense heat from La Caja China is perfect for quick-cooking crispy outsides, while allowing the interior meat to stay moist.

2 lbs ground pork	1 C diced green onion
2 tsp garlic powder	2 Tbs soy sauce
2 tsp brown sugar	1 C shredded lettuce
1 tsp cornstarch	Honey-mustard dressing
16 sesame rolls, split	

Mix all ingredients (except soy sauce) and form 16 equal patties. Brush each patty with soy sauce, and grill over white-ash-covered coals, turning once. Serve with honey mustard and cucumber spears.

Serves 8

I like to chill the seasoned meat and then spread it on an oiled cutting board, using a rolling pin for an even 1/4 inch thickness. Then, I just grab a biscuit cutter, and voila...perfectly round sliders!

Gracie's Luau Pork

Recipe by Perry P. Perkins

While "babymooning" in Hawaii, my wife and I learned the island tradition of throwing a family luau in honor of a child's first birthday. In celebration of our miracle baby, Grace, we hold this traditional feast each year.

4 - bnls pork shoulders (6lb ea)	4 C hot water
1 ½ gal Hawaiian Mojo	2 Tbs seasoned salt
½ C Stubbs liquid smoke	4 Tbs garlic powder
¼ C Adobo Criollo spices	

Marinate pork in Hawaiian Mojo (*pg. 126*) overnight.

Remove from marinade, pat dry, and inject each shoulder with 6-8ozs of remaining marinade.

Score pork on all sides, rub with salt, then brush with liquid smoke, and sprinkle with garlic. Wrap completely in Ti/Banana leaves, tie with string.

The coals should be lit on one side of the covered grill. For gas grills, heat both sides on high, and then turn off one side before loading the shoulder on the cool side.

After the coals are ready, about 45 minutes, place the butts on the grill.

Roast 3 hours, then remove banana leaves.

Toss some apple or alder chips on the coals, and baste with mojo every 45 minutes throughout the rest of the cooking time. The shoulders should not be over any exposed flame.

Cover the grill and vent slightly. Slow cook the shoulders for a total of 6 to 8 hours, until the meat is very tender, or you reach 195 F on the meat thermometer.

Chop the meat and then mix with a wash of 1/2 cup liquid smoke, 4 cups hot water, 1/4 cup Adobo Criollo spices, and 2 Tbs seasoned salt.

Let that sit about 15 minutes, drain remaining liquid, and serve with Sweet Hawaiian Pork Sauce (*pg. 108*)

Traditionally this would be served with white or Hawaiian rice (*pg. 98*)

A nice fruit salad in very complimentary as well.

If you really want to go "Big Island" serve this up with some Lomi-Lomi Salmon, Chicken Long Rice, and Pineapple Haupia.

There are many wonderful Hawaiian cookbooks available, my favorite is "Sam Choy's Sampler."

Serves 40-50

Carolina Pork Ribs

In North Carolina's early days, pork was most commonly cooked over an open fire and seasoned with an ordinary table condiment of the time, which consisted of vinegar, salt, red and black pepper, and oyster juice. Salty vinegar with pepper (but no oyster juice) is basically the same sauce used on most North Carolina barbecue today. The western part of the state usually adds tomato paste of ketchup, as below, for a thicker sauce.

6 racks of pork spareribs	1 ½ C of "Burnin' Love" Rub
1 Qt Carolina Basting Sauce	1 Qt Carolina BBQ Sauce

Prepare ribs by removing the membrane from the underside. Trim off any loose fat, and season ribs with rub, wrap in plastic wrap and refrigerate overnight.

Allow ribs to warm 1 hour. For a charcoal grill, arrange medium-hot coals around a drip pan in a grill with a cover. Place ribs, bone sides down, on the grill rack over pan. Cover and grill for 1-1/2 to 1 3/4 hours or until ribs are tender, brushing with mop sauce every 15 to 20 minutes.

For a gas grill, preheat grill. Reduce heat to medium. Adjust for indirect cooking. Cover and grill as above, except place ribs in a roasting pan.

If you want to sauce the ribs, do so 5 minutes before they're done and watch carefully.

Serves 12-18

Italian Porchetta Sandwiches

Across Italy porchetta is usually sold by pitchmen with their typically white-painted vans, especially during public displays or holidays. Porchetta was introduced to the USA by Italian immigrants of the early 20th century. This is my "smoky" take on this Italian classic.

2 - 8lb pork shoulders, butterflied	6 Tbs fennel Seeds
24 cloves garlic, peeled	Salt & pepper
12 Tbs fresh rosemary	2 C red wine
32 oz sliced pancetta	24 crusty Italian rolls
4 C caramelized onions	6 C Italian parsley

Place the fennel, garlic, rosemary, salt, pepper, wine, and pancetta in a food processor and pulse until well mixed.

Spread the pancetta mixture evenly over the opened pork butt. Roll the pork up firmly, and tie with kitchen twine in four places to hold the pork together.

Wrap in aluminum foil and place in the refrigerator for two days.

You want indirect heat for cooking, you can easily do this on a conventional gas grill.

Just keep the meat as far from the heat source as possible, or it will burn during the long cooking time. You want to cook at 250 degrees Fahrenheit; you can go as high as 275, but no higher.

You don't want to go lower than 250, as you will start to dry out the meat before it's cooked.

Put the shoulder on the "cool side" of the grill, and place a disposable pan with a couple of cups of apple juice underneath it.

A spray bottle with 50/50 apple juice and cider vinegar is nice for basting, as well.

I like to use apple chips, soaked, for smoking. Add ½ cup to a disposable tin pan over the "hot" side of your grill. Refill as needed for the first 3 hours.

After three to four hours, remove the shoulder from your grill, wrap in foil, and roast in a pre-heated oven at 250d for 3-4 hours.

The pork is done when it reaches an internal temperature of 195 degrees.

If you don't have an instant read thermometer (you should really get one) the meat is done when it pulls apart easily with a fork.

Heat the rolls. Place ¼ cup of meat on the warm roll and spoon over a little of the pan juices onto the sandwich.

Top meat with caramelized onions, the ¼ cup of fresh chopped parsley.

Serves 24

Bourbon Pork Tenderloin

The pork tenderloin is usually sold pre-packaged in larger grocery stores. They are often available both plain and flavored with a marinade. Personally, I tend to be distrustful of anyone's marinade but my own!

2 C white sugar	½ C Jim Beam® Bourbon
2 C water	2 tsp vanilla extract
3 to 4 lbs pork tenderloin	2 tsp black pepper
2 tsp garlic powder	2 Tbs salt

In medium bowl, combine sugar, Jim Beam® Bourbon, water, salt and vanilla. Mix well. Place tenderloin in a large zip bag and pour ½ of marinade over the top. Refrigerate 24 hours. Season tenderloin with garlic and pepper.

Prep coals for a two-zone fire and brush the grill with vegetable oil. Remove the tenderloin from the bag and spoon half of sugar mixture over tenderloins.   Place on the "hot" side of the grill and brown to your liking (I like a slight char.)

Move to the "cool" slide of the grate. Cover and cook for 12 to 15 minutes, turning every 1 1/2 to 2 minutes, until the tenderloin reaches an internal temperature of 140 degrees F. Remove the tenderloin from the grill and place on a large piece of heavy-duty aluminum foil folded at the edges to create a basket, and pour on the reserved marinade. Wrap tightly and rest for 10 minutes.

Remove to a cutting board and slice. Garnish and serve.

Serves 8-10

Memphis Whole Pickin' Pig

The first time I cooked a whole pig in my Caja China, my digital thermometer died about fifteen minutes into the process. The good news...I followed the directions printed on the box to a tee, along with the "pig roast worksheet" and the piggie came out perfect!

The only other trouble I ran into was finding out that none of my coolers were big enough to hold the pig, much less the twenty pounds of ice.

Always warn your wife, in advance, that she's going to find a large dead animal in her bathtub...

40-45lb pig, cleaned and butterflied	13oz of table salt
3 C "Burnin' Love BBQ" Rub	½ gallon of water
Memphis Pig Pickin' Mop (pg. 123)	Mesquite liquid smoke
Memphis-Style Barbecue Sauce	Peanut oil
2-3 C fine sea salt	

This recipe is designed for use with La Caja China (the Cuban roasting box.) You can find instructions, online, for pit or rotisserie roasting whole pigs, as well. Plan 1/2lb of raw weight per serving.

Mix up the mop and let it sit at room temperature for 60 minutes or longer. Set aside 4 cups of baste for later use. Mix water and table salt for brine. Then Mix 1 part mop with 3 parts brine.

Inject this combination, an ounce at a time, into the pig every 2-3 inches.

Rinse the pig, inside and out, pat dry. Brush the pig down with oil and then rub all over with the "Burnin' Love BBQ" Rub and some fine sea salt. Put pig back in cooler for 24-36 hours (drain the water, and add ice as needed.).

The day you plan to cook, remove the pig from the cooler and let it warm up to room temperature. This is important for even cooking.

Add 1 cup of mesquite liquid smoke to reserved mop and use this to baste pig before lighting the coals, just before turning, and again after turning.

Then sprinkle the whole pig inside and out with fine sea-salt.

If you're cooking in a pit smoker, or have a La Caja China's with the electric smoker attachment, leave out the liquid smoke and burn some apple wood for the first two hours or so.

Place pig between the racks and tie using the 4 S-Hooks.

Cover box with the ash pan and charcoal grid. Add 16 lbs. of charcoal for Model #1 Box or 18lbs. for Model #2, or Semi Pro Box, and light up. Once lit (20-25 minutes) spread the charcoal evenly over the charcoal grid.

Cooking time starts right now.

After 1 hour add 10 lbs. of charcoal. Continue to add 9 lbs. of charcoal every hour until you reach 195 on the meat thermometer.

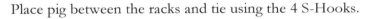

IMPORTANT: Do not open the box until you reach the desired temperature!

Once you reach 195, (3-3 ½ hours) lift the charcoal grid shake it well to remove the ashes, now place it on top of the long handles.

Remove the ash pan from the box and dispose of the ashes.

Flip the pig over, baste again, and replace the cover to crispy the skin.

Flipping is easily done using La Caja China's patented Rack System, just grab the end of the Rack lift and slide as you pull upward, using the other hand grab the top end of the other rack and slide it down.

Score the skin using a knife, this helps to remove the fat and crisp the skin. I just cut a shallow X in each of square of the rack. You want to cut most of the way through the skin, but not into the meat. Cover the box again with the ash pan and the charcoal grid; do not add more charcoal at this time.

After 30 minutes, take a peek, if Ms. Piggy isn't quite as gold and crispy as you wanted, close the lid for another ten. You will continue doing this every 10 minutes until the skin is crispy to your liking.

Once the pig is to your liking, set the lid back on at an angle, so the pig stays warm but isn't cooking, and let it rest for 30-60 minutes...it will still be too hot to touch bare-handed. For easier carving, lay the whole pig, ribs up (on it's back), and use a boning knife to remove the entire skeleton before slicing or chopping the meat.

Serve with warmed sauce, on the side.

Now, I've cooked a LOT of pork-shoulders over the years, but I've never tasted any pork that compared to this. It was sweet and juicy, and the crispy skin was out of the world!

This was the first (of several) pigs I've done in La Caja China, and remember that it was *so* much easier than I thought it would be. With La Caja China, if you can read the instructions printed on the box, you can roast a whole pig!

To make a traditional Cuban roasted pig, follow this same recipe, but substitute Mojo for the Memphis Pig Pickin' Baste, and rub the pig with Adobo Criollo (Cuban style dry rub) instead of the bbq rub.

Be sure to strain the portion of the mojo you intent to inject.

I strongly recommend using Kingsford brand charcoal. All of the recipes on La Caja China's website, as well as in this book, are based on Kingsford. Different brands burn at different temperatures and speeds. Just FYI.

Carolina Pulled Pork Sandwiches

Grandpa Frank's Recipe

1 boneless pork butt (5-6 pounds)
2 Tbs hickory salt
2 cups cider vinegar
1 cup water
2 Tbs salt
1 Tbs red pepper flakes
2 teaspoons ground cayenne

2 Tbs smoked paprika
1 Tbs black pepper
1 cup Southern Comfort
2 Tbs molasses
¼ cup hot sauce
1 Tbs black pepper

In a bowl, combine paprika, hickory salt, 1 Tbs black pepper, and cayenne. Coat pork shoulder with seasonings and cover with plastic wrap. Refrigerate 24 hours.

Preheat grill for medium heat. Place pork shoulder on grill and allow to smoke using soaked (and drained) hickory chips. Place a grill thermometer on the grate to track temperature. Combine remaining ingredients for baste.

Add charcoal and wood chips as necessary to keep temperature at medium, or between 200 - 225°F. Smoke pork shoulder for 5-6 hours or until internal temperatures reach 185°F. Use baste every 20 minutes during the last three hours of cooking. Remember to boil any remaining basting sauce before using it on shredded pork.

Serve on soft white rolls, topped with your favorite coleslaw.

Mom's BBQ Pork Chops

Admittedly, Mom wasn't much interested in cooking, but she had a couple of dishes that, when she decided to cook 'em, they couldn't be beat. This was one of them.

6 boneless pork chops, thick
Pepper to taste
1 cup sweet barbecue sauce

1 Tbs (ea) salt and sugar
1 cup water
1/4 cup cider vinegar

Place chops in a baggie with 1 cup of water, and sugar (boiled and cooled), and brine 4 hours.

Preheat an outdoor grill for high heat.

In a small saucepan, combine barbecue sauce and vinegar. Bring to a simmer and allow to cook 20-30 minutes, uncovered, stirring often.

Brush grate lightly with oil before placing pork chops on the grill. Cook over hot coals for 10 to 12 minutes, turning once. Brush with sauce just before removing chops from grill.

Serve with remaining sauce.

Serves 6

Peach Mojo Pork Shoulder

1 - 6lb pork shoulder	1 qt Hawaiian Mojo (*pg. 126*)
½ cup sea-salt	1 can peach slices, in syrup
2 Tbs garlic powder	2 Tbs red pepper flakes
15 oz sliced peaches in syrup	16 oz peach preserves
12oz apricot & pineapple preserves	
½ cup Stubbs Mesquite Liquid Smoke	

Inject the pork with mojo and marinate overnight. Then, allow pork to come to room temp just before roasting. Brush pork liberally with liquid smoke, then rub all over with sea-salt, garlic, and 1 Tbs of red pepper flakes. Let rest 1 hour.

Glaze: Combine liquid smoke, canned peaches (with syrup), apricot/pineapple preserves, peach preserves, and remaining red pepper flakes. Simmer one hour over medium-low heat. Cool to room temp.

Preheat grill for medium heat. Place pork shoulder on grill and allow to smoke using soaked (and drained) hickory chips. Place a grill thermometer on the grate to track temperature.

Add charcoal and alder wood chips as necessary to keep temperature at medium, or between 200 - 225°F. Smoke pork shoulder for 5-6 hours or until internal temperatures reach 185°F.

Use baste every 20 minutes during the last three hours of cooking. Remember to boil any remaining basting sauce before using it on the pork.

Slice the pork and pile in a pan, slather the top with a generous layer of peach-pineapple glaze and then place pans under a hot broiler for another 5-10 minutes to brown the glaze.

Serve with sweet Hawaiian rolls and white rice.

Serves 12-14

Sweet & Savory Bacon Wrapped Dates

Everything tastes better with bacon, and dates are no exception! Be warned, we serve these as appetizers while the pig or lamb is roasting, and they go fast!

1 lb thick-sliced bacon, cut in half
4 ounces gorgonzola cheese

1 lb pitted dates
32 toothpicks

Slice dates up one side, and open them up. Pinch off a piece of cheese, and place it into the center of the date.

Close the halves of the dates, and wrap a half-slice of bacon around the outside, secure with a toothpick.

Lay a single sheet of foil over La Caja China grill grates, and add the wraps in a single layer.

Grill until bacon starts to crisp, then flip each wrap over.

When the second side is crisped, remove to a platter lined with paper towels, allow to cool slightly, and then get the heck outta the way, 'cause folks will trample you to get them!

Jalapeño Pepper Bombs

Recipe by Chris Renner

These bite-sized bombs are always a hit. Roasting take a bit (but not all) of the fire out of the peppers, and leaves a sweet, smoky, spicy treat that will have your guests begging for more.

10 fresh jalapenos	20 Cheddar Lit'l Smokies
8oz. Cream Cheese	2 Lbs. Bacon (½ strip ea)
1/8 Sweet Onion (diced)	1 Tbs. Sugar

Soften cream cheese and blend in sugar and onions.

Slice Jalapenos in half, lengthwise, and trim away all seeds and membranes, rinse. Spoon 1 teaspoon of cream cheese mixture into each side. Place 1 smokie on each half, and press it into the cream cheese.

Wrap each pepper half in bacon, securing each with a toothpick.

Lay a single sheet of foil over La Caja China grill grates, and add the bombs in a single layer. Grill until bacon starts to crisp, then remove to a platter lined with paper towels.

Allow to cool slightly, and serve.

If these "bombs" have too little kick heat for you, use a whole pepper for each. Clamshell the cream cheese and smokie in the pepper and wrap the whole wonderful thing in bacon. This is how Chris Renner does it, but he's a lot tougher than I am. - Perry

Finned Favorites

(fish & seafood)

Simple Grilled Oysters

Garlic Asiago Oysters

Burnin' Love Wasabi Oysters

Fish Camp Trout

Southern-Grilled Bass

Unagi Salmon & Grilled Pineapple

Pacific Northwest Salmon w/Lemon Dill Sauce

Seared Wasabi Tuna

Bacon Grilled Crappie

Soft-shell Crabs

Mojo Shrimp Skewers

Sweet Lobster Tails

Sturgeon Kabobs

Grilled Clams

How to shuck a raw oyster

This is the snack that keeps the cook going…in the kitchen, I mean!

Rinse oysters in cold running water before opening. Hold oyster cup side down and hinge pointed toward you.

Insert oyster knife at hinge slowly but firmly and push the knife between the shells.

Use a slight side to side rocking movement with your knife as you push in.

Work tip of knife into the oyster (about 1/2 inch), and twist the handle to pop oyster open. Slice muscle from top shell.

Open top shell, and cut muscle from bottom cup. Leave the oyster in the bottom cup, being careful not to spill the liquor. Turn the meat over for most professional appearance.

Top with 1-teaspoon cocktail sauce and ¼ teaspoon wasabi mustard.

Slurp!

If you're having trouble getting your oysters to "sit up straight" on the grill, you can fashion some small rings out of aluminum foil to place each oyster in, while it's cooking.

Simple Grilled Oysters

For generations before the pioneer settlers arrived, Chinook Indians gathered oysters around what is now Willapa Bay and camped in the area that is now Oysterville, Washington.

The heat from the grill steams the oysters and pops the shells open, while poaching the oyster inside.

4 dozen oysters, scrubbed
1 C butter
1 tsp lemon pepper

Lemon wedges
1 Tsp seasoned salt

Melt butter with seasoned salt and lemon pepper

Place oysters, unshelled, on grill. Oysters have a "cup" side (like a bowl) and a "lid" side (flat), the cup side should be down so as not to lose all the yummy juices.

Get your condiments close to the grill on another table and make sure everyone has put on their gloves. Have aluminum pie pans available, if you like, to use as plates. When shells open (in about 3 minutes), use an oyster knife to detach oyster from top shell, and plop it back into the cup with the hot oyster liquor. Discard the lid.

Then, encourage everybody to dig in, topping oysters with their favorite condiments, or seasoned butter. Continue cooking the oysters in batches until they're gone.

Oysters that don't open should be discarded.

Garlic Asiago Oysters

1 lb sweet cream butter
2 dozen fresh oysters
French bread, warmed

1 Tbs minced garlic
½ C grated Asiago cheese
¼ cup chives, diced

Light coals or start grill, heat to medium high.

Melt butter over medium-high heat. Reduce heat to low, and stir in garlic.

Cook 1 minute, and remove from heat.

Place oysters, cup down, on grill. As soon as shells pop open, remove from grill.

Shuck oysters, keeping as much of the oyster liquor in place as possible.

Cut connective muscle and return each oyster to its shell.

Drizzle each oyster with 2 teaspoons butter mixture and sprinkle with 1 teaspoon cheese. Grill over high heat 3 minutes or until cheese browns. Sprinkle with chives.

Remove from heat, and serve immediately with bread and remaining butter on the side.

Burnin' Love Wasabi Oysters

We get our organically grown oysters hand-harvested from Oysterville Sea Farms on Washington's Willapa Bay. The combination of a spicy-hot sauce and the steaming brine of a fresh grilled oyster is amazing.

12 small Pacific oysters, raw in shell
8 oz white wine
2 Tbs wasabi mustard
1 C unsalted butter, cubed
salt and black pepper to taste

2 Tbs white wine vinegar
1/4 C shallots, minced
1 Tbs soy sauce
1 C chopped cilantro leaves

In a saucepan, over medium heat, combine the white wine vinegar, wine and shallots. Simmer until the liquid is slightly reduced.

Strain out shallots and discard, return liquid to the pan. Reduce heat to low.

Add wasabi mustard and soy sauce, stirring.

Over low heat, gradually whisk in butter. Do not let the mixture boil.

When all of the butter has been incorporated, stir in cilantro, and remove from heat. Pour into a small bowl, and set aside.

Prepare a dish of coarse salt to hold the oyster shells in place.

Clean oysters thoroughly. Place oysters, flat side up, on a grill preheated to medium, and close the lid. Cook oysters until shells just open (5-6 minutes).

Remove oysters from the grill and cut muscles from the top shell, (careful – don't spill the liquor.)

Turn the oyster over and return it to the cup half of shell. Discard the lid.

Press each oyster (in shell) into the coarse salt to keep it upright, then spoon 1-2 teaspoons of wasabi-butter sauce over each and serve immediately.

Be prepared to cook a lot of oysters!

Fish Camp Trout

As a avid fly fisherman, born and raised in the Pacific Northwest, I've eaten a lot of trout in my time. No, seriously... a LOT of trout. This simple recipe remains one of my very favorites. Whether it's on my grill at home, or over a sage fire on the banks of the Deschutes, it really doesn't get much better than this.

4 small whole trout, cleaned
4 sprigs of fresh thyme
salt and pepper to taste

4 strips of bacon
1 lemon

Oil and preheat grill. Fry bacon, so that it's started to cook, but is still soft. Rinse out the trout and pat dry with a paper towel.

Place a sprig of thyme inside each fish. Wrap each trout with a strip of bacon and secure with a toothpick.

Place trout on grill or in an oiled grill basket, and grill 5-7 minutes per side depending on the size of the trout. The trout is done when the meat turns opaque in the center and easily flakes. Discard bacon, squeeze a little fresh lemon juice over each fish, and serve.

Chris with dinner

Serves 2

Southern-Grilled Bass

Okay, this is one of those recipes that just sounds…weird. You're gonna have to trust me.

2 lbs. bass fillets or steaks
1 qt. mayonnaise
6 oz. soy sauce

Mix mayonnaise and soy sauce.

Cover entire surface (meat side) of each bass fillet with mixture.

Place on charcoal grill, skin-side towards heated coals. Do not turn.

When edges turn up and scales flake, remove and serve.

Serves 6

Unagi Salmon & Grilled Pineapple

Unagi (sometimes called Sushi Sauce) can be found in most Oriental stores, or specialty aisles.

If you're a sushi fan, you've probably had this thick, rich, slightly sweet sauce served with your caterpillar roll.

This last minute experiment turned into my all-time favorite grilled salmon recipe.

1 fresh salmon fillet, skin on (about 3lbs)
2 Tbs minced scallion
¾ C Unagi sauce (also sold as Sushi Sauce)

2 Tbs toasted sesame seeds
1 teaspoon minced garlic
½ C good olive oil

Light briquettes and brush the grilling rack with oil to keep the salmon from sticking.

While the grill is heating, lay the fillet on a cutting board and cut it crosswise into six equal pieces. Whisk together the Unagi, olive oil, and garlic. Generously brush half the mixture onto the salmon and allow it to sit for 10 minutes.

Place the salmon skin side down on the hot grill; discard any marinade the fish was sitting in. Grill for 4 to 5 minutes, depending on the thickness of the fish. Turn carefully and grill for another 5 minutes. The salmon will be slightly raw in the center, but don't worry; it will keep cooking as it sits.

Transfer the fish to a flat plate, skin side down, and spoon the reserved marinade on top. Allow the fish to rest for 10-15 minutes. Top with sesame seeds and scallions, and serve warm (not hot) with grilled pineapple (see next page.)

Many salmon recipes direct you to throw away the skin just before serving the salmon. Good lord, the crispy grilled skin is the most flavorful part of the fish!

Simple Grilled Pineapple

There are lots of sauces that can be brushed on pineapple for grilling, but I like this simple sauce that doesn't overpower the flavor of the fruit.

Obviously, this recipe is better with fresh pineapple slices, but most folks have better access to canned, so I made it with that.

1 can pineapple (sliced)
1 Tbs honey
1 tsp lemon juice

3 Tbs butter (melted)
1 Tbs brown sugar

Combine all ingredients and microwave 1-2 minutes. Stir until mixed in evenly.

Use a small kitchen brush and coat pineapple slices. If you don't have a kitchen brush, then get a big baggie. Pour in the sauce. Roll the pineapple slices gently. (Fresh pineapple will stand up to a bit more abuse than canned.)

Put the slices on the grill. Heat (medium hot) until you see grill marks (3 to 6 minutes depending on the heat).

Turn and grill the other side.

Remove from the grill and serve.

Serves 6

Pacific Northwest Salmon
with Lemon Dill Sauce

Described and enthusiastically eaten by the Lewis and Clark Expedition, the Chinook salmon is spiritually and culturally prized among certain Native American tribes.

Many celebrate the first spring Chinook caught each year with "First Salmon" ceremonies.

This heavy, flavorful fish is named for the Chinook Indians - master traders and fishermen who are now almost gone from the face of the earth, but once enjoyed a peaceful existence along the Columbia River and Northwest Coast.

(2) 6lb Chinook salmon fillets	Salt to taste
1 C butter, melted	1 C lemon juice
4 Tbs dried dill weed	1 Tbs garlic salt
Black pepper to taste	4 C plain yogurt

Place salmon fillets in a baking dish.

Mix the butter and 1/2 lemon juice in a small bowl, and drizzle over the salmon. Season with salt & pepper.

Combine yogurt, dill, garlic powder, sea salt, and pepper. Spread sauce evenly over salmon.

Quickly wipe hot grill grate with a towel dipped in a little canola oil, place fillets on grill, tent with foil, and close lid.

Grill fish, skin down, to medium rare, about 6 minutes. (Fish should be well colored on the outside and barely translucent at the center.) or until salmon is easily flaked with a fork.

Plate and spoon extra sauce over the top.

Serve with wild rice.

Seared Wasabi Tuna

Chris Renner, and his father Bob, catch our tuna, and grill it in camp fresh from the Tillamook Bay in Garibaldi, Oregon.

The tuna is seared but not cooked all the way through. Use sushi quality tuna because you'll want to leave the center very rare.

Of course, you can decide how cooked you want it.

(6) 6-ounce tuna steaks
1 cup cilantro leaves
1/4 cup shallots, minced
1 tablespoon wasabi paste
1 tablespoon olive oil

1 1/4 cup white wine
1 cup unsalted butter
2 Tbs white wine vinegar
1 tablespoon soy sauce
salt and pepper to taste

Combine wine, wine vinegar and shallots in a saucepan over medium heat. Simmer to reduce to about 2 tablespoons. Strain out the shallots and discard.

Add wasabi and soy sauce to mixture and reduce the heat. Slowly add butter while stirring until completely mixed. Stir in cilantro and remove from heat. Set aside.

Preheat grill as hot as you can get it. You really need a lot of heat for this one. Brush tuna steaks with olive oil. Season with salt and pepper and place on grill.

Grill for 90 seconds then turn and continue grilling for 90 seconds more. If you just want the tuna seared remove from grill now. Otherwise continue grilling for 1 minute on each side again.

Serve with sauce.

Bacon Grilled Crappie

Again, let's face it...everything's better with bacon! These are one of the best "in camp" appetizers I've ever had.

20 Crappie Fillets
20 Bacon Slices
¼ teaspoon garlic powder
¼ teaspoon onion powder
¼ teaspoon pepper

Sprinkle spices on fillets. Roll up fillets, wrap with bacon and peg with a toothpick. Grill over very low charcoal heat, turning fillets several times.

Be sure to put out all flames caused by bacon grease with a water spray bottle.

Cook until bacon is brown and inside of fillet flakes.

This can also be done in the oven broiler, but be sure to use a drip pan for the bacon grease.

Soft Shell Crabs

As crabs grow, their shells cannot expand, so they molt the exteriors and have a soft covering for a few of days when they are vulnerable and considered usable as soft-shells. A New England staple, the sweet and subtle briny flavor of fresh soft-shell crab is truly the essence of the sea. They're good little monsters!

24 jumbo soft-shell crabs
4 tsp black pepper
4 tsp Hot Sauce

4 tsp salt
1 ½ C butter
4 Tbs lemon juice

Remove the eye sockets and the lower mouth. Remove the gills. Gently rinse with cool water and pat them dry. Sprinkle the crabs with the salt and pepper.

Melt butter with hot sauce and lemon juice and stir to mix. Remove from the heat and cool for several minutes. Toss crabs with butter sauce and let sit for 20 minutes.

Frill over a medium-hot fire, covered for four minutes. Flip, cover, and cook for about five minutes or until the crabs are slightly crusty.

Baste with the butter sauce and serve.

Serves 24

Mojo Shrimp Skewers

One warning about roasting a whole pig....for the last forty-five minutes of cook time, there's an ever-expanding cloud of mouth-watering aroma that will gather friends, family, and neighbors you've never met, in seagull-like crowds to your yard. The best way to deal with these culinary paparazzi, is to toss the grill racks over the coals and prepare a few simple, tasty appetizers.

One of my favorites is bacon-wrapped mojo shrimp, inspired by La Caja China's special Adobo Criollo spice blend. Simple to prepare, you can assemble dozens of these skewered treats between the time you fire up the roaster, and the time the aroma of yummy goodness begins wafting through your neighborhood.

2 lbs sliced bacon

2 C Traditional Cuban Mojo

32 skewers, soaked

64 raw prawns, tail off

¼ C Adobo Criollo

Rinse raw prawns and drain. In a large bowl, toss prawns and Adobo Criollo spices.

Wrap each prawn in ½ slice of bacon, and thread two wraps onto each skewer, touching, and with skewer through both the bacon and the shrimp. Once your coals have turned completely white, but before adding unlit charcoal, lay skewers in grill, with only the meat over the coals.

Grill 3-5 minutes, until bacon is cooked, flip, and cook 2-3 more minutes.

Remove from grill and let rest on a paper-towel covered platters 2-3 minutes before serving. for this type of grilling.

Sweet Grilled Lobster Tails

A surf-n-turf dinner with grilled fresh lobster tails and filet mignon is a surefire hit.

This grilled lobster is perfect for any occasion. If you don't have a lot of experience grilling shellfish, then this easy recipe is for you. Lobster tails only take a few minutes to grill, so wait until your steaks, or other entree are done cooking before grilling lobster tails.

12 lobster tails	½ C olive oil
¼ C fresh lemon juice	½ C butter
1 Tbs crushed garlic	1 tsp sugar
1/2 tsp salt	½ tsp black pepper

Combine lemon juice, butter, garlic, salt, and pepper over med-low heat and mix until well blended, keep warm. Create a "cool zone" with minimal coals at one end of the grill. Brush the meat side of tails with olive oil, place onto grill and cook for 5-7 minutes, depending on the size of the lobster tail. Make sure to turn once during cooking process.

After turning, baste meat with garlic butter 2-3 times. The shell should be bright red when they are finished. Remove the tails from the grill, and using large kitchen shears, cut the top part of the shell open.

Serve with warm garlic butter for dipping.

Sturgeon Kabobs

Sometimes referred to as "poor man's lobster" because of its sweet, succulent meat, the massive sturgeon is a prehistoric survivor of the ice age, and the largest freshwater fish in the world. Ancient Romans believed sturgeon to be an aphrodisiac with life-extending properties.

While I can't make any promises about your love life, I guarantee that these kabobs will be the hit of your next barbecue!

4 lbs raw sturgeon	4 lbs sliced bacon
12 metal double-skewers	2 bottles of Teriyaki sauce
4 cans pineapple chunks (optional)	

Cut sturgeon into 1-inch cubes. Wrap a half slice of bacon around it, and skewer, making sure to pin the bacon, as well as the meat, (so the bacon won't fall off.)

Alternate pineapple and bacon wrapped sturgeon, until skewers are full.

Place filled skewers in a baking dish and pour the teriyaki sauce over them, turning to coat well, and let sit for 1 hour.

Place skewers on your grill, over white coals, and baste with sauce while cooking.

Cook 8-10 minutes, turning and re-basting once. Do not allow the bacon to burn.

If you're using wooden skewers, make sure you soak them for about 20 minutes before grilling.

63

Grilled Clams

If the Northwest cockle clam ever becomes an endangered species (it won't) it will likely be the fault of my friends, the Shores. Dane and Michelle have two obsessions, adopting at-risk kids, and scouring the low-tide stretches of the Oregon Coast until they've collected their family limit in cockles.

They swear that there is no correlation between the two. Whatever. Beautiful things like Dane's grilled clams, and Michelle's clam chowder are sure to follow. One word of warning - around the Shores' house...don't be late for dinner!

2 dozen sm cockle or cohog clams
1 pound sweet butter, melted
2 tsp fresh minced garlic

1 cup olive oil
1 lemon, juiced
2 tsp minced Italian parsley

Inspect the cockles to ensure the shells are closed. Since clams live in sand, they need to be thoroughly rinsed under cold water several times to rid the shell of debris.

Combine butter, lemon juice, garlic and parsley in food processor, keep warm beside your grill. Grill clams over medium coals. Cover with foil, or close the grill lid and steam the clams 2-3 minutes, checking often, until the shells have just popped open.

Dredge each open clam in the butter mixture and set back on the grill. Cook 1-2 minutes longer.

Plate cockles and add salt.

Feathered Friends

(chicken & turkey)

Southern Roast Turkey

Giblet Gravy

TurCraCon

Spatchcocked Garlic Chicken

Burnin' Love Beer Can Chicken

Flattened Mojo Chicken

Lazy Legs Chicken

Competition BBQ Chicken

Sizzlin' Buffalo Wings

Peanut Chicken Satays

Peking Duck

Southern Roast Turkey

Adapted from my father's, Chef Frank L. Perkins, recipe.

1 16lb turkey, frozen
Smoked paprika
1 ½ C salad oil
3 C white sugar

Salt and pepper to taste
1 C melted butter
3 C fine sea salt

Boil 4 cups of water with 3 cups of fine sea salt, and 3 cups white sugar.

Allow to cool. Pour seasoned water into a 5-gallon bucket. Put your frozen turkey in the bucket, and fill with water until totally submersed. Put a weight on the turkey to hold it down. Cover your bucket with a towel and leave it like that overnight.

Rinse the turkey and pat it dry. Turn the wings back to hold neck skin in place. Return legs to tucked position. Brush the turkey with oil. Season with paprika, salt and pepper, inside and out. Place the turkey, breast side down, on a wire rack in a large heavy-gauge foil pan.

Place the pan on the grill, away from the source of heat. Close the lid.

Cook for 11 to 13 minutes per pound, until the turkey registers an internal temperature of 165°F (74°C) in the thigh and 170°F (77°C) in the breast.

Remove the turkey from grill and allow to rest 30 minutes before carving and serving.

Serve with your favorite stuffing and Turkey Giblet Gravy (see next page.)

Yee-Haw!

Terry Ramsey carvin' the bird in camp

To collect drippings for making gravy, pour a little water into the foil pan. Replenish the water as needed to keep the drippings from burning. Remove pan from beneath the turkey about 30 minutes before the bird should be done and make gravy. Continue cooking the turkey directly on the grate.

Turkey Giblet Gravy

Giblets from 1 turkey, rinsed.
½ tsp powdered sage
¼ C diced celery
¼ C turkey fat
3 C turkey broth

1 tsp garlic, minced
¼ C diced onions
2-3 C water
½ C flour
1 C milk

Boil giblets and remove from water (save.)

Dice and sauté in oil with a little garlic, sage, diced onion, salt, pepper, and diced celery. Add 1 cup of water and giblets, simmer until liquid is almost gone.

Repeat until giblets are tender.

To make the gravy, pour the turkey fat into a pan, over medium heat.

Gradually whisk the flour into the fat, until smooth, and cook for about five minutes, stirring constantly.

Slowly whisk in 4 cups of liquid (2 cups stock, 1 cup water & boiled giblets, 1 cup milk). Stirring constantly, bring to a boil, then reduce to simmer until thickened, about 5 minutes.

Add giblet mixture, season with salt and pepper to taste, and serve.

Thanks, Dad!

TurCraCon

Tur(key) Cra(nberry) & (Ba)Con roll.

Okay, so I wanted to come up with something unique for Thanksgiving, and, of course, I wanted to incorporate barbeque in the process. Unfortunately, I have a dirty little secret...I don't really like smoked turkey all that much. Something I do love, however, is the Bacon Explosion™ — the pork-wrapped torpedo of yummy goodness. With that vision of fatty loveliness firmly in my mind, I took my basic recipe and decided to transform it into a Thanksgiving goodie, modifying the basic ingredients of the holiday.

My lovely wife, Victoria, named this dish for me, winning the contest on my blog. Every time I say it, I have to overcome the urge to bellow, "Release the TurCraCon!"

1 pound sliced bacon	1.5 pounds ground turkey
1 cups breadcrumbs	1/2 sweet onion, diced fine
1/4 lb Mushrooms. sliced thin	2 stalks celery, diced fine
2 Tbs fresh minced garlic	1/4 cup sweet cream butter
1/4 cup rub *(pg 119)*	3/4 cup cranberry barbecue sauce *(pg. 109)*
1 tablespoon each sage, garlic powder, salt, pepper	

Mix ground turkey with 1 tablespoon each sage, garlic powder, salt, pepper. Refrigerate 2-3 hours.

Using 10 slices of bacon, weave a square lattice like that on top of a pie: first, place 5 bacon slices side by side on a large sheet of aluminum foil, parallel to one another, sides touching. Place another strip of bacon on one end, perpendicular to the other strips.

Fold first, third and fifth bacon strips back over this new strip, then place another strip next to it, parallel to it. Unfold first, third and fifth strips; fold back second and fourth strips. Repeat with remaining bacon until all 10 strips are tightly woven. (The instructions are a lot more complicated that the actual process!) Sprinkle with some of the rub.

Preheat oven to 225 degrees or light a fire in an outdoor smoker. Sautee onion, celery, minced garlic, and mushroom in butter until wilted but still crisp, drain. Toss with breadcrumbs and a little additional salt and pepper, press and cool. You want the mixture to still be fairly dry.

Evenly spread ground turkey on top of the bacon lattice, pressing to within 1/2 inch of the outer edges of the bacon. Sprinkle with rub. Spread a thin layer of stuffing mixture over the ground turkey, pressing to 1/2 inch of the outer edges of the turkey.

Very carefully separate front edge of sausage layer from bacon weave and begin rolling sausage away from you, rolling the stuffing into the center. Bacon weave should stay where it was, flat.

Press turkey roll to remove any air pockets and pinch together the seams and ends to seal.

Roll turkey toward you, this time with bacon weave, until it is completely wrapped. Turn it so seam faces down. Roll should be about 2 to 3 inches thick.

Place roll on a baking sheet in oven or in smoker. Cook until internal temperature reaches 165 degrees on a meat thermometer, about an hour per inch of thickness.

When about 30 minutes from done, glaze the roll with sauce. To serve, slice into 1/4- to- 1/2-inch rounds. Serve on potato rolls with a side of warmed Cranberry Barbeque Sauce. (*Pg. 109*)

Mashed potatoes and turkey gravy make a nice Thanksgiving accompaniment.

Serves 10

Spatchcocked Garlic Chicken

A flattened, or "spatchcocked" chicken cooks in less time than a regular chicken and can be grilled or roasted without becoming overcooked.

1 - 4 pound young chicken
2 Tsp ground pepper
4 cloves minced garlic

1 Tbs sea salt
4 Tbs olive oil

Place chicken breast side down and using poultry shears cut out the backbone. Spread the two sides apart and press down on the breast so that the chicken lies flat.

Combine olive oil, garlic, and pepper.

Wash the chicken in cold water, and pat dry. Rub chicken with oil/spice blend, and drop into a gallon-size plastic bag. Refrigerate overnight.

Build a charcoal fire on one side of your grill; if using a gas grill leave one side unlit, cover and preheat for 20 minutes. Place chicken skin side down at the edge of the fire with legs closest to the heat. Watch carefully and turn over when skin starts to brown. Move chicken to the side of the fire and cover with a large disposable aluminum pan (a favorite restaurant trick.) The grill cover can be used, but the browning and flavor will be less intense.

Cooking time will vary, depending on the fire and the size of the chicken. Check the temperature at 20 minutes after turning. When the temperature in the thigh reaches 175, remove from the heat and let sit, covered, for 15 minutes before carving.

Burnin' Love Beer Can Chicken

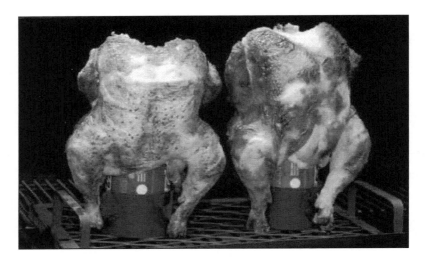

This is another of my all time favorite recipes. If you're not excited about using beer, a soda can filled with apple juice is lovely, too.

If this becomes one of your favorites as well, do what I did and invest in a "Double Can" roasting rack. Cheap, easy to clean, and much more stable that just the can.

> 1 large whole chicken (4 to 5 pounds)
> 3 tablespoons rub (recipe below)
> 1 12-ounce can of beer

Rinse the chicken, inside and out, under cold running water; then drain and pat dry. Rub 1 tablespoon of the rub inside the body cavity; then another tablespoon all over the skin. Rub another half-tablespoon between the flesh and the skin.

Cover and refrigerate the chicken overnight.

Open a can of beer. Pour out a couple of inches of beer; then, using a screw driver, carefully poke several holes around the top of the can.

Pour remaining dry rub into the can.

Holding the chicken upright (legs pointed down), insert the beer can up into the chicken. *Insert junior-high boy's locker-room humor here.*

Oil the grill grate. Stand the chicken up in the center of the hot grate, over the drip pan. Spread out the legs to form a tripod, to support the bird.

Cover the grill and cook the chicken about an hour. Use a thermometer to check for doneness. The internal temperature should be a minimum 170 degrees.

Using tongs, lift the bird to a cutting board or platter, allowing the beer can to slip out onto the grill. Be careful, the contents of the can are VERY hot. An assistant with a second set of tongs is helpful here.

Let stand for 5 minutes before carving.

Serves 6

As an Oregonian, it's my civic responsibility to remind you NOT to toss the beer can out along with the carcass. Please empty, rinse, and recycle.

Beer-Can Chicken Rub

This is a simple, easy to make rub that is pretty darn good with just about anything. You rub enough of this on an old boot, and it wouldn't be half bad.

> 1/4 cup coarse sea salt
> 1/2 cup light brown sugar
> 1/4 cup smoked paprika
> 2 tablespoons freshly ground black pepper

Combine all ingredients and mix with your fingers. Store the rub in an airtight jar away from heat and light. Good for at least 6 months.

Makes about 1 cup

Flattened Mojo Chicken

Mojo [MOH-hoh] is considered the signature marinade of Cuba, and is used to complement a wide variety of foods such as beef, pork and poultry.

3 - 4lb whole chickens   3 Tbs olive oil

6 C Traditional Cuban Mojo (*pg. 125*)   3 tsp. sea salt

3 Tbs Adobo Criollo spice blend

Rinse chicken with cold water and pat dry. Cut out backbone with kitchen shears.

Turn chicken breast side up and open like a book. Press down firmly on breast to flatten and break rib bones. Loosen skin from body under breast and thighs.

Place each chicken in a gallon-size resealable bag with 2 cups Mojo. Marinate (flat) in refrigerator 24 hours.

Remove chickens from bags and discard mojo. Blot each bird dry, and rub each with 1 Tbs olive oil, and then 1 Tbs Adobo Criollo spice blend.

Build a charcoal fire on one side of your grill; if using a gas grill leave one side unlighted, cover and preheat for 20 minutes. Place chicken skin side down at the edge of the fire with legs closest to the heat.

Watch carefully and turn over when skin starts to brown. Turn and move chicken to the side of the fire and cover with a large disposable aluminum pan (a favorite restaurant trick.)

The grill cover can be used, but the browning and flavor will be less intense.

Cooking time will vary, depending on the fire and the size of the chicken. Check the temperature at 20 minutes after turning;

When the temperature in the thigh reaches 175 degrees, remove from the heat and let sit, loosely covered for 15 minutes.

Halve, quarter, or carve the chicken and serve with Saffron Basmati Rice.

Serves 9

Both Cuban Mojo and Authentic Cuban Adobo Criollo can be purchased directly from La Caja China at www.lacajachina.com (under "Mojo & Spices.")

Lazy Legs Chicken

This is one of the best (and easiest) barbecue recipes you're ever likely to find...

1 "Family Pack" Chicken legs or thighs
1 bottle Yoshida's Original (or your favorite Oriental grilling sauce.)

Combine chicken and sauce in a gallon-size resealable bag and allow to marinate 8-12 hours, turning several times.

Start a two-zone fire with a cool area in the middle.

Grill chicken over hot-zones until browned on both sides, then move to cool area, and cover with foil pan.

Cook, turning once until done, 10-15 minutes.

Serve with sticky rice and stir-fly veggies.

Serves 6-8

This recipe is awesome with boneless chicken thighs, too. When cooked, just slice and serve as a rice bowl. Boil the marinade 10-15 minutes, stirring, and top!

Competition BBQ Chicken

Both bone-in and boneless chicken are awesome on the grill. Bone-in will take more time to cook, but many pitmasters argue that leaving the bones in adds greatly to the flavor.

Personally, I believe this as well. The secret is to sear the chicken over direct heat to retain juices and then finish cooking with indirect heat. This is a recipe I used a few years back at a local chicken competition.

I didn't win...these things are all politics!

2 whole chickens, cut up	¼ cup olive oil
2 tsp salt	1 cup bottled bbq sauce
¼ cup cider vinegar	¼ cup brown sugar, packed
2 Tbs hot sauce	

Clean the chicken and prepare the grill. Brush chicken pieces with olive oil and season with salt. When the coals are white, spread them evenly over one-half of the grill area. If using gas, turn off one burner after the grill is preheated. Place chicken skin side down directly over the hot coals or gas flame and cover the grill.

Cook until the skin is seared; turn and sear the other side. Keep the grill covered while cooking, but watch for flare-ups. Keep a spray bottle handy. When both sides are seared, remove chicken to the "cool" side of the grill to finish cooking over indirect heat.

Brush the chicken with sauce. Turn every 10 minutes or so and brush with sauce again until the chicken is done with an internal temperature of about 160° F.

Boneless breasts will cook thoroughly in only 15-20 minutes. Meaty, bone-in pieces will require 35-45 minutes of cooking over medium-low heat. When the chicken is done, place over direct heat for a few minutes to caramelize the sauce and add deeper color if desired.

Serves 6

Sizzlin' Buffalo Wings

This is pretty close to the original spicy Buffalo chicken wings recipe from the Anchor Bar, in Buffalo NY, where they first appeared in October, 1964. The recipe has been modified slightly for the grill.

36 chicken wings, separated
1 tsp salt
1 ½ Tbs white vinegar
¼ tsp garlic powder
¼ tsp Worcestershire sauce
6 Tbs Frank's Red Hot Sauce
celery sticks

1 Tbs vegetable oil
1 C all-purpose flour
¼ tsp cayenne pepper
1 tsp Tabasco sauce
¼ tsp seasoned salt
6 Tbs unsalted butter
blue cheese dressing

Mix all except chicken, salt, oil and flour in a pan, bring to a simmer, stirring, and then cool.

Toss the wings with the oil, and salt. Place into a large plastic bag, add the flour, and shake to coat evenly. Remove from the bag, shaking off excess flour.

Place wings on hot grill, turning several times until golden brown.

Remove wings from grill and place them in a sealed bowl with the sauce and shake well.

Serve immediately with blue cheese and chilled celery sticks.

Peanut Chicken Satays

Satays are and Asian-inspired street food that pack a lot of flavor onto a small stick.

Traditionally a grilled skewer with pieces of seasoned meat, seafood or even tofu, these are like the "New York Hotdog" of the Pacific Rim. The bite-size chunks make satays easy to eat, and they work just as well as an appetizer as they do a main course.

4 Tbs olive oil	4 Tbs sesame oil
2 tsp ginger powder	2 tsp powdered garlic
2 Tbs curry powder	Butter lettuce leaves
20 wooden skewers, soaked	Fresh cilantro leaves
2 lbs chicken thighs, cut into strips	

Peanut sauce:

2 C chunky peanut butter	½ C soy sauce
1/4 C brown sugar	¼ C sweet chili paste
1/3 C limes juice	2/3 C hot water

Combine oils, ginger, garlic, and curry powder in a shallow mixing bowl.

Place the chicken strips in the marinade and gently toss until well coated.

Cover and let the chicken marinate in the refrigerator overnight.

Thread the chicken pieces onto the soaked skewers working the skewer in and out of the meat, down the middle of the piece, so that it stays in place during grilling.

Brush grill with oil to prevent the meat from sticking.

Grill the satays for 3 to 5 minutes on each side, until nicely seared and cooked through.

Serve on a platter lined with lettuce leaves and cilantro; accompanied by a small bowl of peanut sauce on the side.

For the sauce:

Combine the peanut butter, soy sauce, chili paste, brown sugar, and lime juice in a food processor or blender. Puree to combine, and drizzle in the hot water to thin out the sauce.

Pour the sauce into individual serving bowls.

If you're serving this as a main dish, add a side of steamed jasmine rice, and fresh veggies.

Peking Duck ala La Cajita China

The dish, originally named "Shaoyazi," was mentioned in the Complete Recipes for Dishes and Beverages manual in 1330 by Hu Sihui, an inspector of the imperial kitchen. Beijing's most famous dish, Peking Duck is traditionally served with Mandarin pancakes.

I've modified this dish slightly for roasting in La Cajita China.

(2) 5 to 6 pound ducks	12 cups water
¼ C powdered ginger	6 scallions, cut into halves
½ C honey	¼ C rice wine vinegar
½ C sherry	Scallions for garnish
6 tablespoons cornstarch	1 C Hoisin Sauce

Clean ducks. Wipe dry and place each duck on a "beer-can chicken" stand. Set in a cool room in front of a fan for 4 hours to dry, turning every 30 minutes.

Bring the water to a boil, and add ginger, scallion, honey, vinegar, and sherry. Boil 10 minutes, then pour in the dissolved cornstarch, stirring constantly.

Place one duck in boiling water for five seconds and remove. Place the second duck in boiling water for five seconds and remove. Repeat for 10 minutes.

Place ducks on "beer can" racks again, in front of fan, for 6 hours until thoroughly dry. Turn every 30 minutes.

"Pre-heat" La Cajita China with 10lbs of charcoal. When all coals are covered in white ash, oil the pre-heated roasting rack and place ducks, breast side up, on rack.

WARNING – Edges of the box will be *very* hot, be careful not to touch them when placing the ducks inside.

Place the rack in the roasting pan with 2 inches of water in bottom, and close up the box, and add another 5lbs of charcoal. You goal temperature inside the box is 350 degrees. Roast 20 minutes.

Turn ducks, add 5lbs of charcoal, and roast 20 minutes more. Turn breast side up again. Roast 5 minutes more, until crispy and browned to your liking. Remove ducks from La Cajita China and allow to rest 10-15 minutes.

Use sharp knife to debone. Serve meat and skin immediately on a pre-warmed dish.

The duck is eaten hot with hoisin sauce and rolled in Mandarin Crepes. Garnish with diced scallion.

Each duck serves 3 to 4

SUPER SIDES

Frijoles Negros (Black Beans)
Sautéed Butter-Rum Plantains
Vickie's Favorite Brisket Beans
Smothered Sweet Corn
Pop Fairrington's Hor-De-Voors
Cebollas Curtidas (Pickled Onions)
Hawaiian Rice
Whole Hog Dirty Rice
Ma Geisert's Cheesy Potatoes
Savory Watermelon Salad
Quick Saffron Rice
Mac n' Cheese

FRIJOLES NEGROS

(black beans)

2 lbs. black beans
20 C of water
1 green pepper
1 C olive oil
1 large onion
8 garlic cloves
4 Tbs sugar

2 bay leaves
8 tsp. salt
1 tsp. pepper
1 tsp. oregano
4 Tbs. vinegar
4 Tbs. olive oil
1 C red wine

Wash the beans and soak in water. When the beans swell, cook in the same water until soft. (45 minutes.)

Heat the oil in a frying pan, add onion, chop up or mash garlic and chop up green pepper. Add 1 cup of the beans to the pan and mash. Add this to the beans together with the salt, pepper, oregano, bay leaves and sugar.

Allow to boil for a 1 hour then add the wine and vinegar allowing to cook uncovered for a while.

Add 4 tbs. of olive oil just before serving.

Serves approximately 20

Sautéed Butter-Rum Plantains

Plantains are a staple food in the tropical regions of the world, treated in much the same way as potatoes and with a similar neutral flavor and texture.

2 C dark rum	1 C dark brown sugar
Salt	2 Tbs butter, diced
1/4 cup canola oil	6 very ripe plantains

Peel and slice plantains on the bias, 1/2-inch thick. Plantains should be very ripe (almost black.)

In a heavy skillet, melt the butter over medium heat. Add half of the plantains and fry them in a single layer for about 4 minutes on each side.

Remove with a slotted spoon and keep warm in a bowl. Repeat.

Drain and wipe oil from the same pan, combine the rum, brown sugar, butter, and salt. Stir over medium heat until the sugar has dissolved, then bring the mixture to a vigorous boil.

Cook for 2 minutes, until slightly thickened.

Return the plantains to the pan and stir to coat them evenly with the sauce.

Allow to cool slightly, and serve.

Serves 6

Vickie's Favorite Brisket Beans

This is a great "next day" recipe after serving smoked brisket. My BBQ partner Chris saves the burnt ends from his briskets specifically for this recipe. Make sure you save the broth from the brisket pans as well. Chill it overnight and skim off the excess fat before adding to this recipe.

1-lb smoked brisket, cubed
1 C chopped onion
1 C brown sugar bbq sauce*
2 Tbs yellow mustard
16oz kidney beans, drained
16oz butter beans, drained
16oz diced tomatoes, drained

10 slices bacon, diced
1 C brown sugar
¼ C hot sauce
1 tsp chili powder
1 tsp black pepper
28oz baked beans
2 cups brisket broth

Sautee onions & bacon, add brisket cubes to warm.

Add all remaining ingredients (except beans), simmer 30 minutes.

Add beans, mix gently, and transfer into a heavy baking dish.

Bake at 350 for 1 hour, uncovered.

---

*I typically brew up my own sauce, but in case of emergencies - my preferred bottled brands for this recipe are Sweet Baby Rays Brown Sugar BBQ®, and Frank's Red Hot Sauce®.

Pop Fairrington's Hor-De-Voors

Okay, these don't really have anything to do with barbecue, per se, but they're so dang good, I just had to add them. Pop Fairrington made them up for us at elk camp one year, with his own smoked salmon, and I've been addicted ever since!

    5 oz smoked salmon, diced
    8 oz pineapple cream cheese
    2 whole avocados,
    20 Ritz crackers

Dice the salmon. Pit and cube avocados, then sprinkle pepper and garlic.

Take a cracker, spread with cream cheese, place a chunk of salmon on one half, and a chunk of avocado on the other.

Try to stop eating them…good luck.

Pop Fairrington hauls in a nice one!

Pineapple cream cheese can be tricky to find, but you can make your own with a small can of crushed pineapple, a little sugar, and 8oz of cream cheese. Make sure that you press as much liquid as possible out of the pineapple, or your cream cheese will end up runny.

Smothered Sweet Corn

Maque choux, also called smothered corn, is a traditional dish of southern Louisiana that has a heavy Native Indian influence due to the corn that is used with it. It is believed that the Indians had a similar recipe, and that the Cajuns added to it. Maque choux is usually served as a side dish, but it can also be used as a focal point of a main dish.

> 2 C sugar
> 1 large red onion, chopped
> 1 medium bell pepper, chopped
> 2 lg tomatoes, diced
> 1 gallon whole kernel corn, drained
> 2 sticks butter, salted
> ¼ C fresh Italian parsley, chopped

In a large pot (preferably cast iron), melt the butter.

Add the sugar and cook over medium heat until the mixture starts to turn a light brown. Add onion and bell pepper, and sauté for 2 minutes.

Add the corn and tomatoes. Stir often to prevent it from sticking to the bottom.

Cook until the mixture becomes a golden brown. This may take up to 45 minutes.

Toss with fresh parsley and serve.

Serves 25-30

Tomatillo Salsa Verde

Recipe by Dane Shores

This authentic, Mexican salsa verde has a fabulous flavor. Use it on barbacoa tacos, brisket, or as a condiment for any dish that needs a little extra zing! Serve with warmed tortilla chips, or, if you're having me over…just a spoon.

1 pound tomatillos, husked
1/2 cup finely chopped onion
1 teaspoon minced garlic
1 Serrano chile peppers, minced
2 tablespoons chopped cilantro
1 tablespoon chopped fresh oregano
1/2 teaspoon ground cumin
1 1/2 teaspoons salt, or to taste
2 cups water

Place tomatillos, onion, garlic, and chile pepper into a saucepan. Season with cilantro, oregano, cumin, and salt; pour in water. Bring to a boil over high heat, then reduce heat to medium-low, and simmer until the tomatillos are soft, 10 to 15 minutes.

Using a blender, carefully puree the tomatillos and water in batches until smooth.

Cebollas Curtidas
(pickled onions)

Cebollas curtidas (pickled onions) is a simple , yet elegant way of preparing onions for the perfect combination of sweet and sour to complement any savory or spicy meal.

4 large red onions, peeled and halved
2 C fresh lime juice
Salt

Thinly slice the onions and place into a heat-proof, non-reactive bowl.

Pour boiling water over them, wait 10 seconds, then pour the onions into a large strainer.

Return the drained onions to the bowl, pour on the lime juice and stir in the 1 ½ teaspoons salt.

Cover and place in the refrigerator until serving time.

Before serving, taste and season with additional salt if you think necessary.

Makes 7 cups

Hawaiian Rice

From the mid 1860's when the whaling industry's domination of Hawaii's economy ended, until the 1920's, rice was second in value and acreage only to sugar cane in the Hawaiian Islands.

The islands of Kauai and Oahu proved most suitable to rice cultivation, because of their abundance of water.

2 ½ C jasmine rice	5 C chicken stock
1 ½ C diced pineapple	2 C diced ham
6 Tbs. butter	Salt & pepper
½ C slivered almonds	Dash red pepper flakes

Cook rice in chicken stock until stock is absorbed.

Brown pineapple and ham in butter.

Stir in rice and season, to taste, with salt and pepper.

Add almonds, stir well and bake for 15 minutes in a 350 degree oven.

Serves 8-10

Whole Hog Dirty Rice

This recipe is one of the reasons I love roasting whole pigs in La Caja China. The broth is simply amazing, with a richness that is impossible to get with any smaller cut of pork.

1 lb roasted pig, chopped
1 Can cream of mushroom soup
2 "cans" reserved pork broth

2 stalks celery, minced
1 C raw jasmine rice
1 sweet onion, minced

Combine raw rice, veggies, and soup in a heavy pan. Use the empty soup can to add broth.

Cook covered at medium approximately 90 minutes, or until rice is cooked.

Stir once or twice while cooking

Add chopped, roasted pork during last 5 minutes of cooking.

Serves 4-6

Ma Geisert's Cheesy Potatoes

Recipe by Shar Geisert

As the one who hung the nickname "Bubba" on me, I owed it to my good friend Shar "Ma" Geisert to include this fabulous dish. She served this one holiday dinner...and owned me from that point on. A quick and simple recipe with amazing results!

1 stick butter	1 can cream of chicken soup
1 C cheddar cheese, shredded	¼ C chopped sweet onion
1 ¾ C sour cream	2lbs frozen cubed hashbrowns
Salt & pepper	

Preheat oven to 350d

Melt the butter, mixing in all of the ingredients except the hashbrowns.

Once combined, add hashbrowns.

Spray a 13x9 pan, add all this stuff, and bake 1 hour & 15 minutes, or until potatoes are brown and crunchy on the edges.

A handful of cooked, diced bacon, or some freshly roasted red bell paper can be added for a nice twist.

Savory Watermelon Salad

Recipe by Terry Ramsey

Our BBQ partner-in-crime, Terry Ramsey, grills this refreshing treat as a side dish or dessert. It's always a hit!

5 lbs seedless watermelon
Extra-virgin olive oil
60 sm basil leaves, torn
1 C goat cheese, crumbled
¼ C green onion, chopped

¼ C balsamic vinegar
Coarse sea salt
Fine black pepper
¼ C white sugar
16 cherry tomatoes, halved

Slice watermelon into 1-inch thick cubes.

Pour the vinegar into a small saucepan with sugar, and bring to a simmer over medium-high heat.

Cook until reduced to a thick syrup consistency. Set aside.

On the "cool end" of a 2-zone fire, grill watermelon about 2 minutes per side, until grill marks appear. Transfer to a plate and season with salt.

Combine all ingredients into salad plates and finish each salad with a very light drizzle of olive oil and balsamic syrup, and chopped onions.

Dust with black pepper and serve immediately.

Quick Saffron Rice

Saffron rice is a favorite side dish to roast chicken in Thailand. This quick (and fat free) recipe uses a bit of turmeric to balance the much more expensive saffron.

2 C Thai jasmine rice	3 ½ C chicken stock
½ tsp salt	½ tsp turmeric
½ tsp saffron threads	1 clove garlic, minced

Pour stock into a medium-size pot, and heat on high.

While stock is coming to a boil, add the turmeric, saffron, and garlic. Stir well. Add the rice and stir. Return to a boil, then reduce heat to low and cover tightly with a lid.

Cook 12-15 minutes, or until the rice has absorbed the liquid, then turn off the heat.

Allow to sit 5-10 minutes, or until you're ready to eat. The residual heat inside the pot will finish steaming the rice, and the rice will stay warm in this way for an hour or more.

Before serving, remove the lid, fluff rice with a fork, and taste-test before adding salt.

> *To check for doneness, insert a butter knife straight down into the pot and push the rice aside. If you see liquid, it still needs more time to cook.*

Mac n' Cheese

Recipe by Cassia Hobbs

Macaroni is mentioned in various medieval Italian sources, though it's not always clear whether it's a noodle or a prepared dish. It was apparently considered an upper-class dish even in Italy until around the 18th century. Its popularity in the United States has been attributed to Thomas Jefferson for serving it at a White House dinner in 1802.

4 Tbs butter	2 clove garlic, minced	2 C Panko
4 Tbs flour	3 cups milk	½ cup oil
1½ cup heavy cream	10oz cheddar, shredded	2 tsp garlic salt
1 tsp salt	10oz Monterrey jack, shred	¾ tsp dried parsley
Dash hot sauce	16oz macaroni pasta	½ tsp pepper
1 tsp pepper	2 Tbs grated parmesan	

Melt butter in large sauce pan. Sweat garlic in butter before adding flour to make roux (medium thick). Add milk and cream slowly at first stirring briskly to keep roux from becoming chunky. Bring milk mixture to a simmer and add cheese, stirring to let cheese melt. Add salt, pepper, and hot sauce to taste.

Cook noodles in salted water to al dente. Cool and toss with oil (optional).

Pour noodles into baking dish. Pour cheese sauce over noodles, you will want it to look like you have way more sauce than noodles. Top with panko mixed with oil and seasonings. Bake in a 325 oven for 15-30 min until sauce is bubbling and bread crumbs are browned.

Enjoy!

Tasty Toppers
(sauces, rubs, & mops)

North Carolina BBQ Sauce

Memphis-Style Barbecue Sauce

Texas Brisket Sauce

Sweet Hawaiian Pork Sauce

Cranberry Barbeque Sauce

Spicy Thai Peanut Sauce

Garlic Mojo

Gorgonzola Dipping Sauce

Perry's Secret "Burnin' Love" Rub

Smokey Beef Rib Rub

Hellfire Cajun Rub

TurCraCon Rub

Carolina Basting Mop

Basic Vinegar Mop

Perry's Pig Pickin' Baste

Traditional Cuban Mojo

Hawaiian Mojo

North Carolina Barbecue Sauce

In the Carolinas, the barbeque meat is pork, and the barbeque sauces are matters of hot debate even from one town to the next. Some sauces are thin and vinegary, while some regions add ketchup, or even mustard. This is the recipe I grew up with.

1 qt cider vinegar	12 oz ketchup
2/3 C packed brown sugar	2 Tbs salt
¼ C lemon juice	1 Tbs red pepper flakes
1 Tbs smoked paprika	1 Tbs onion powder
1 tsp each: black pepper, dry mustard	

Bring all ingredients to the boil, and then simmer for 30-45 minutes, stirring frequently. Allow to cool, and serve or bottle.

Okay, if you promise not to tell my customers, I'll let you in on a little secret...

When I run out of my homemade bbq sauce, and my Caja and I are running late to an important date, there are a couple of "off the shelf" sauces that I'm willing to pair with my favorite recipes...

Sweet Baby Rays® (brown sugar), or Stubbs Mesquite®.

Memphis-Style Barbecue Sauce

Memphis barbecue sauce has its own distinctive flavor, as well. Though the specific ingredients will vary from cook to cook, Memphis sauce is usually made with tomatoes, vinegar, and any countless combination of spices.

Memphis sauce is poured over pulled pork or served along side of dry ribs.

1 Tbs butter	¼ C finely chopped onion
1 ½ C ketchup	¼ C chili sauce
4 Tbs brown sugar	4 Tbs molasses
2 Tbs yellow mustard	1 Tbs fresh lemon juice
1 Tbs Worcestershire sauce	1 Tbs liquid hickory smoke
½ tsp garlic powder	½ tsp salt
½ tsp ground black pepper	1 tsp chili powder
dash cayenne pepper	

Bring all ingredients to the boil, and then simmer for 30-45 minutes, stirring frequently.

Allow to cool, and serve or bottle.

Texas Brisket Sauce

Texas is famous for tender slow-smoked brisket. Sauces are usually thin, spicy, and mixed with intensely flavorful pan drippings.

½ C brisket drippings (defatted)
1 Tbs Worcestershire sauce
½ tsp hot pepper sauce (Franks)
2 cloves of garlic, pressed
½ tsp chili powder

½ C vinegar
½ C ketchup
1 lg onion, diced
1 Tbs salt
Juice of one lemon

Combine all ingredients.

Simmer, stirring occasionally, for 15 minutes.

Allow to cool and refrigerate 24-48 hours before using.

Sweet Hawaiian Pork Sauce

Kalua Pork (or pig) is one of my favorite Hawaiian dishes. It's a smoky, salty pulled pork dish served over white rice, with a variety of optional sauces - from a simple liquid smoke and water wash, to elaborate sauces that highlight the tropical fruits and sugar cane of the islands.

15oz peaches & juice
16oz peach preserves
2 Tbs liquid smoke
1 Tbs red pepper flakes

15oz pineapple & juice
1 cup brown sugar
2 Tbs minced garlic

Combine all and bring to boil.

Lower heat and simmer on low until sauce has begun to thicken.

Keep warm until serving. Drizzle over pulled pork.

For a very classy presentation, shred the pork, top with whole pineapple rings, baste well with sauce, sprinkle generously with crushed macadamia nuts, and return to La Caja China 5-10 minutes to brown the top.

Cranberry Barbeque Sauce

This sweet/tangy cranberry bbq has just a hint of heat from the Jalapeno pepper (how's that for some alliteration?), and lends itself very well to the mildness of turkey. I think it would be a very nice glaze for chicken as well. If you serve additional cranberry barbeque sauce on the side, go sparingly. It's very rich, and too much will quickly overpower the flavor of the meat

1 Can Cranberry Sauce (jellied).
1/4 Cup Brown Sugar
1/2 Jalapeno, seeded, rinsed, and finely diced
1/4 Cup Orange Juice
1/4 Cup Ketchup
1/4 Cup Apple Cider Vinegar
1 Tsp Yellow Mustard

Empty cranberry sauce into 2-quart saucepan blender, add the remaining ingredients, whisk, and cook, over medium heat, until simmering.

Cook until the mixture is thick. Rest overnight if possible.

Makes 2 cups

Spicy Thai Peanut Sauce

This easy peanut sauce has a terrific authentic Thai taste. It is spicy and peanutty, and is perfect as a dipping sauce for chicken, shrimp, and beef.

        3 C creamy peanut butter
        3/4 C coconut milk
        1/3 C fresh lime juice
        1/3 C soy sauce
        1 Tbs fish sauce
        1 Tbs hot sauce
        1 Tbs minced fresh ginger root
        5 cloves garlic. minced

In a bowl, mix the peanut butter, coconut milk, lime juice, soy sauce, fish sauce, hot sauce, ginger, and garlic.

Simmer 10 minutes, and serve.

Garlic Mojo

Mojo (pronounced mo-ho) is the Spanish name for a number of Latin sauces made with vinegar or citrus juice and garlic.

It is a traditional accompaniment to the starchy root vegetables of the Hispanic Caribbean, as well as a marinade for pork, chicken, and other local meats.

> 8 garlic cloves
> 1 tsp salt
> 1/4 C sweet orange juice
> 1/8 C of fresh lime or lemon juice.
> 1 Habanero pepper, diced (optional)

Chop garlic fine with salt, or crush using a mortar and pestle or food processor with salt to form a thick paste.

Wearing gloves, carefully core Habanero pepper and wash out all seeds and membranes. Dice pepper, set aside. Wash prep area, dispose of gloves and wash your hands with dish soap.

In a mixing bowl, combine the garlic paste, pepper, and juice, and let the mixture sit at room temperature for 30 minutes or longer.

Gorgonzola Dipping Sauce

Blue cheese is believed to have been discovered by accident. The caves in which early cheeses were aged shared the properties of being temperature and moisture controlled environments. Gorgonzola, a favorite of mine, is one of the oldest known blue cheeses, having been created around 879 AD

1 C crumbled blue cheese
2/3 C sour cream
½ C mayonnaise
1 clove garlic, minced
1 oz white wine
2 tsp Worcestershire sauce
1 tsp salt
1 tsp fresh ground black pepper

In a glass or plastic bowl, combine all ingredients, using the salt and pepper to finalize the taste and the white wine to set the consistency.

What is a Rub?

In the food of the Southern United States, dry rub is often used on grilled or barbequed meats.

Dry rubbed ribs are a popular dish, but steaks, burgers or pork chops are also given flavor through a spice rub.

Most typical Southern style spice rubs include chili and cayenne pepper, garlic and onion powder, salt and black pepper, paprika and dry mustard.

Although the quantities of hot ingredients can be adjusted, rubs are often an extremely spicy mix that add a powerful kick to meat.

Perry's "Burnin' Love" Rub

"Burnin' Love BBQ" is the name of the catering business that my fellow pit-masters, Chris Renner, Terry Ramsey, and I operate. Really, it's just an excuse to stand around in smoke and cook a lot of pigs and briskets…but don't tell our wives, okay?

This is our secret pork shoulder rub. Apply it generously to the inside of a butterflied shoulder, roll it, tie it, and apply more rub to the outside. You MUST allow the rubbed shoulder to rest in the fridge at least overnight so that the rub will help form that wonderful "bark" while roasting.

Finally, after it's done cooking and you've pulled, chopped, or shredded the meat, give it one last sprinkle for an intense, spicy flavor.

> ¼ C coarse sea salt
> ¼ C light brown sugar
> 2 Tbs garlic powder
> 2 Tbs onion powder
> 2 Tbs Italian seasonings (spicy, if you can find them)
> 4 Tbs smoked paprika
> 2 Tbs coarse black pepper
> 1 Tbs hickory salt
> 1 tsp cayenne powder

Mix well.

Good for 6-8lbs of pork.

Renner's Amazing Brisket Rub

Christopher Renner is the unquestionable brisket king of our team, and possibly anywhere else on the planet, as well. His rub recipe is as simple as it is wonderful...

For 4 full briskets (7-8lbs each):

    1 C fine sea salt
    1 C coarse pepper
    1 C granulated garlic
    1/4 C smoked paprika

Rub briskets and refrigerate 12-24 hours.

Allow briskets to come to room temp before smoking.

Smoke brisket(s) with a combination of oak and pecan wood chips or pellets, at a temp between 200-225.

Jonathan Renner - brisket man in training...

Chris says that the difference between good brisket and amazing brisket is patience.

Double wrap the finishing brisket in foil, wrap that in a towel, and let the whole thing rest in a closed cooler for 1-2 hours.

Then, once you've unwrapped it, allow it to sit and cool slightly for 15-20 minutes for slicing or pulling.

Smokey Beef Rib Rub

2 Tbs brown sugar
2 Tbs black pepper
2 Tbs smoked paprika
2 Tbs chili powder
2 tsp onion salt
2 tsp garlic powder
2 tsp celery salt
2 tsp seasoning salt

Mix well and rub both sides of ribs, wrap tightly in plastic wrap, and refrigerate overnight.

Bring ribs to room temperature before cooking.

Hellfire Cajun Rub

Dry rubs can be applied to meat, fish, or poultry or added to pasta, jambalaya, or any dish that you want to spice up. This rub makes a great seasoning for fried, baked, or grilled chicken, as well.

8 Tbs smoked paprika	4 Tbs cayenne powder
4 Tbs dried parsley	4 Tbs black pepper
2 Tbs garlic powder	6 Tbs fine sea salt
2 Tbs ground cumin	4 Tbs dried oregano
1 tsp ghost chili powder (to taste)	

Combine all the ingredients, mix well an store 24-48 hours, in an airtight container, before using.

Wear gloves, and use extreme caution, when handling ghost chili powder, even breathing the tiniest amount will be painful.

This chili has been measured at over 1 million Scoville units (by comparison, Jalapeno peppers are about 4500 Scoville units.)

This is the hottest Chili Powder available anywhere.

Start with just a teaspoon...trust me.

TurCraCon Rub

2 Tbs coarse sea salt
1 Tbs garlic powder
1 Tbs smoked paprika

1 Tbs coarse black pepper
1 Tbs dry mustard
2 Tbs white sugar

Mix all ingredients together, and store in an airtight container.

Keep in a cool, dark place.

A Word About Mops

Barbecue "Mops" or basting sauces, are vinegar (or other) based liquids that are applied to meats during the slow cooking process of traditional barbecue, to keep the meat moist and add flavor.

Legend has it that President Johnson liked his barbecue, and often called upon is favorite Pitmaster to cook for hundreds of guests. The meal would be cooked on a forty square-foot open air fire pit. The cook would cover every inch of this in ribs, briskets, halved pigs, and just about any other meat he could think of.

To keep all that meat moist he mopped it with a thinned sauce...using a real mop. Hence the barbecue term, "mop."

Today you can buy a miniature tool that looks like a kitchen mop to mop your meat. the cotton fibers hold the thin mop sauce and make it easy to dash large amounts on at once. If you ask the barbecue experts, they'll tell you that rubs and mop sauces are key to every Championship BBQ team.

Carolina Basting Mop

Mopping (basting) the meat while cooking helps keep it moist and adds additional flavors. Never use a basting brush on any meat that has a dry rub applied, as it will brush off seasonings.

Mop the meat every 30 minutes for the first half of the cooking time.

2 qts Water
2 qts Apple Cider Vinegar
2 qts vegetable oil
1 C liquid smoke
½ C salt
¼ C cayenne pepper
¼ C black pepper
1 sweet onion, diced fine

Combine all ingredients and bring to a simmer. Allow to cool overnight, and warm before using.

Use as a rib/chicken baste, or sprinkle on pulled or chopped pork before serving.

Basic Vinegar Mop

2 C cider vinegar
½ C vegetable oil
5 tsp salt
4 tsp red pepper flakes or powder

Combine all ingredients and bring to a simmer, allow to cool overnight to help the flavors marry.

Keep warm and apply to meat before you close La Caja China, when you flip the meat, and again when the meat is done cooking.

Allow the meat to rest at least 30 minutes to soak up the mop.

Perry's Pig Pickin' Mop

This recipe is for the whole hog, but in reality, it can be used for all types of pork. If you're preparing smaller cuts of pork, simply scale back the quantities. Use as a marinade, and injection, a mop, and finally, as a wash on the finished meat, just before serving.

1 qt. apple juice	1 qt. apple cider vinegar
¼ C fine sea salt	¼ C garlic powder
¼ C smoked paprika	1 C light oil
1 tsp black pepper	1 tsp cayenne pepper
½ C mesquite liquid smoke (unless you have smoker)	

Simmer for 15-20 minutes.

Keep warm and apply to pig before you close La Caja China, when you flip the pig, and again when the pig is done cooking.

For a more traditional "Eastern" North Carolina mop, use only the apple juice, vinegar, salt, and cayenne. For South Carolina, add 1 cup prepared mustard to that.

Beef Rib Mop

3/4 C brown sugar
1/2 C bottled barbecue sauce
1/2 C ketchup
1/2 C cider vinegar
1/2 C Worcestershire sauce
1 C water
1 Tbs salt
1 Tbs chili powder -- optional
1 Tbs paprika

Combine all ingredients in a quart jar. Shake to blend thoroughly.

Best if made ahead of time; will keep indefinitely in the refrigerator.

This mop is great for brisket, as well. Keep warm and apply to ribs before you close La Caja China, when you flip the ribs, and again when the ribs are done cooking.

Makes 1 quart

Traditional Cuban Mojo

Recipe by Roberto Guerra

This classic Cuban seasoning sauce makes a flavorful marinade for meats and poultry. Traditionally this is made with sour oranges, cumin, lots of garlic. With larger cuts (pork shoulder, or whole pig & lamb) it can be injected into the meat 12-24 hours before cooking.

1 C sour orange juice
1 Tbs oregano
1 Tbs bay leaves
1 garlic bulb
1 tsp cumin
3 tsp salt
4 oz of water

Peel and mash the garlic cloves. Mix all the ingredients and let it sit for a minimum of one hour.

For marinade, add the above recipe to 1 ½ gallons of water, and 13 oz. of table salt.

Blend all ingredients and let it sit for a minimum of one hour, strain and inject, or place meat in a cooler and pour marinade to cover overnight.

You can replace the sour orange juice with the following mix: 6 oz. orange juice, 2 oz. lemon juice.

Hawaiian Mojo

This is my variation of Roberto's Cuban Mojo. "Real" luau pig is typically seasoned with just salt and liquid smoke. I like the sweet, Polynesian overtones that this marinade/mop adds to the pork.

1 C orange juice
1 C pineapple juice
½ C mesquite liquid smoke
1 Tbs oregano
1 Tbs minced garlic
1 tsp cumin
3 tsp salt
4 oz. of water

Mix all the ingredients and let it sit for a minimum of one hour.

For marinade/injection, add the above recipe to 1 ½ gallons of water, and 13 oz. of table salt.

Blend all ingredients and let it sit for a minimum of one hour, strain and inject, or place meat in a cooler and pour marinade to cover overnight.

After injecting/soaking the pig or shoulder, apply a salt rub all over the meat, use Kosher salt or coarse sea salt.

Approximate Servings Per Pound

(Raw weight)

Pork, Shoulder Bone-in	3
Pork, Back Ribs	1.5
Pork, Country Style Ribs	2
Pork, Spareribs	1.5
Pork, Whole	1.5
Beef, Standing Rib	2.5
Beef, Ribs	2.5
Beef, Tri-Tip	4
Chicken, Whole	3
Lamb, Leg (bone in)	1
Turkey, Whole	¾

When planning a meal, it is always better to purchase too much meat than not enough.

Always be prepared for people with larger appetites.

One trick I use is to add a "mystery" guest for every 4 confirmed. In other words, I plan 5 portions for 4 people, 10 portions for 8, 15 for 12, etc.

If there are leftovers, the cooked meat will keep in the refrigerator for several days or the unused portions may be frozen for long term storage.

Wood Smoking Chart

Wood type	Characteristics	Use with
Alder	Very delicate with a hint of sweetness.	Good with fish, pork, poultry, and light-meat game birds. Traditionally used in the Northwest to smoke Salmon.
Apple	Slightly sweet but denser, fruity smoke flavor.	Beef, poultry, game birds, pork (particularly ham).
Cherry	Slightly sweet, fruity smoke flavor.	Good with all meats.
Hickory	Pungent, smoky, bacon-like flavor.	Good for all smoking, especially pork and ribs.
Maple	Mildly smoky, somewhat sweet flavor.	Good with pork, poultry, and small game birds
Mesquite	Strong earthy flavor.	Most meats, especially beef. Most vegetables.
Oak	The second most popular wood to use. Heavy smoke flavor. Red Oak is thought the best by pitmasters.	Good with red meat, pork, fish and heavy game.
Pecan	Similar to hickory, but not as strong.	Good for most needs.
Cherry	The flavor is milder and sweeter than hickory.	Good on most meats.
Black Walnut	Very heavy smoke flavor, usually mixed with lighter wood like pecan or apple.	Good with red meats and game.

More Recipes

Look for more tasty recipes on out blog: www.burninloveblog.com!

Including...

Low Carb BBQ Sauce

Tri-Tip Sliders with Garlic Provolone Sauce

Grilled Buffalo Liver & Balsamic Onion Sandwich

Grilled Sea Bass with Caviar Sauce

"Fully Awe-some" Burgers

The Krispy Kreme Bacon Cheeseburger

Dad Perkins' Shrimp N' Grits

Hangtown Fry (Eggs & Oysters)

Pico de Gallo

Terry's Sweet & Spicy Jalapeño Lemonade

Chicken Nuggets with Unagi Dipping Sauce

Cuban Pork Sandwiches

Pineapple Upside-down Spam Cake

Italian Stuffed Pork Tenderloin Appetizer

Simple Tangy Coleslaw

...and many more!

INDEX

About the Authors

Terry D. Ramsey, Perry P. Perkins, Christopher Renner

Perry P. Perkins comes from a long line of professional chefs. As a third generation gourmand, he focuses his love of cooking on barbeque, traditional southern fare, and fresh Northwest cuisine. A freelance writer, Perry's books are available at your favorite online bookstores.

Terry D. Ramsey is our resident baker. An accomplished chef, Terry's first love (and special gift) is baking the breads and sweets that accompany every barbeque dish we serve. When a slice of cake melts in your mouth, when a bite of cornbread makes your eyes roll and your lips whistle Dixie...thank Terry!

Chris Renner is an avid hunter and outdoorsman, Chris prepares wild game and Northwest specialties with patience and a creative flair. Our "brisket-man," Chris has spent decades perfecting his 12-hour Texas brisket, the centerpiece of our barbeque menu.

For more great recipes, tips, and bbq blather, be sure to visit our blog:

http://www.burninloveblog.com

Made in the USA
Middletown, DE
18 December 2018